# Your MA in Theology

# Your MA in Theology

Zoë Bennett
with Carol Reekie and Esther Shreeve

scm press

Published in 2014 by SCM Press
Editorial office
3rd Floor
Invicta House
108–114 Golden Lane,
London
EC1Y 0TG

SCM Press is an imprint of Hymns Ancient & Modern Ltd
(a registered charity)
13A Hellesdon Park Road
Norwich NR6 5DR, UK

www.scmpress.co.uk

British Library Cataloguing in Publication data

A catalogue record for this book is available
from the British Library


978-0-334-04491-8


Typeset by Regent Typesetting, London
Printed and bound by
CPI Group (UK) Ltd, Croydon

# Contents

For Alison and Chris

# Acknowledgements

My grateful thanks are due to all my colleagues in the Cambridge Theological Federation and Anglia Ruskin University with whom I have worked on master's programmes since 1995. Within the Federation there are those with whom I have worked particularly closely and who are unfailingly supportive: Rowena Small, our Registrar; Mat Ridley, our IT expert; Ela Lazarewicz-Wyrzykowska, Amy Barnett and Emma Rothwell, successively our MA Assistant Directors; Carol Reekie and Magda Fletcher, our librarians; Cindy Wesley, the MA Christian Theology Course Leader.

Especial thanks go to Carol Reekie and Esther Shreeve for their enormously helpful contributions to this book on using the library and on specific learning difficulties respectively.

And finally, to Chris Wright and Alison Burling, who have since 1995 successively shared the adventure of developing the MA programmes, borne the burden of holding them together administratively, have been my closest colleagues and have put up with all my faults, I dedicate this book to you with love and gratitude.

Warm thanks are also due to Natalie Watson at SCM Press for encouragement in conceiving and preparing this book, to Rebecca Goldsmith at SCM for help in preparing the text, to Neil Whyte for copy editing and Claire Ruben for proofreading it as well as to Abigail Humphries Robertson for indexing.

# Biographical Information

**Zoë Bennett** is the Director of Postgraduate Studies in Pastoral Theology at Anglia Ruskin University and in the Cambridge Theological Federation. She directs an MA course in Pastoral Theology and a Professional Doctorate in Practical Theology. Her research interests include the use of the Bible in practical theology and the work of the nineteenth-century art and social critic John Ruskin.

**Carol Reekie** is the Cambridge Theological Federation librarian. She has over 30 years' library experience in public, special, further education and higher education libraries. She undertook her master's by distance learning at Aberystwyth University and her part-time PhD research with Loughborough University.

**Esther Shreeve** worked as Church Historian and academic manager in various capacities within the Cambridge Theological Federation for many years. She became interested in dyslexia because of the high proportion of theological students who presented with difficulties, and eventually trained with Dyslexia Action as a specialist teacher and assessor. She now works as a freelance dyslexia tutor and consultant in Edinburgh and can be contacted at comistondyslexia@gmail.com.

# Introduction

'What I enjoyed most was the context of each seminar group as a unique laboratory of sharing and exchange – of ideas, views and theological perspectives.' I treasure this comment from Razvan, an Orthodox student from Romania on our MA in Pastoral Theology. It seems to me to encapsulate the richness master's study in theology can bring, whether we do this in class or by distance learning, full-time or part-time. The richness doesn't only come from the mix of students but from the teaching style that is normally adopted at this level and, of course, from the subject matter itself: 'Most enjoyable is the teaching style (not didactic), which enables you to engage with the subject through discussion, reading, presentations and so on – that is, it is interactive' (Jon, pioneer minister).

Not all is plain sailing, however: 'Perhaps the most difficult aspect has been the frustration of limited time' (Carmen, Methodist student minister from Australia); or as Rita, a Christian educator in her 60s said, the most difficult thing was 'when my thinking about good educational practice differed from the model employed by a module leader'. Time is something most of us realize will be an issue when we study for a master's degree. Perhaps we anticipate some other hurdles less clearly, such as the fact that many of us are already professional people and may experience dissonance between our student status and the skills we bring into the programme.

Studying for a master's in theology can be life-transforming, and some of the difficulties in themselves become ways of growing. Emma, an Anglican ordinand, wrote that one of the most difficult things was:

> juggling the busy life of being a student training for ordained ministry, in a full-time lecturing job and having children – literally! *Yet again, the dual process of studying and having children inspired my authentic voice to speak up a bit more.* (My emphasis)

This book is for people like Razvan, Jon, Carmen, Rita and Emma – people like you. It is primarily about helping you to become more skilled in studying. The book is also for those who teach on master's programmes in theology. Knowing what helps students helps teachers to help students. It all started when I led a day in Cambridge for tutors on our MA in Pastoral Theology on how to supervise and mark MA dissertations. 'Can you recommend something for us to read further on this?', they asked. 'The trouble,' I said, 'is that the MA student is neglected. There are many books on studying at undergraduate level; many on being a research student; but the MA is a poor relative caught in the middle.' This is a great shame, as master's courses in all kinds of theology are burgeoning at the moment, and the needs of master's students are very specific – not the same as undergraduate or research students.[1] You are unique.

Master's courses in theology have many names – Pastoral, Practical, Applied, Contextual Theology; Spirituality, Liturgy or Leadership; indeed one of our MAs in the Cambridge Theological Federation is called simply Christian Theology. I hope this book will be useful to you whichever you are doing. My own background

---

1 Studyportals listed 119 Religious Studies and Theology master's courses in the UK on 13 August 2013 (www.studyportals.eu).

and inclination is to a reflective practice model of practical theology, and that may show through. I hope you can rejoice in that or forgive it, as appropriate. But this book isn't only for one sort of student or for one sort of theology. You will find chapters suitable for international students, for those bringing together theory and practice, for those who have trouble writing or for those who want to look at how Christian commitment might engage with a critical university environment.

You should therefore pick and choose what to read in this book. It doesn't have to be read from beginning to end or read in any particular order. Dip in and look at the aspects of studying your MA that most interest or trouble you at the moment. Some of the chapters address specifically theological issues; others apply more generally, but even these are set in a theological context.

Chapter 1 is about expectations. I begin by asking what it means to study on a 'taught master's'. This chapter covers the difference between undergraduate and postgraduate work, how to cope with return to study after a long gap and how to harness and value your previous academic work and your previous experience. It looks at what is expected academically at master's level. How much 'teaching' should you expect in a 'taught' degree, and how do you learn to study independently?

Chapters 2 and 3 are about basic realities. What are core study skills for master's students? Reading? Writing? (but not Arithmetic unless you do quantitative research for your dissertation). Then there is the art of taking notes and the art of reflection. How do you use the libraries and search for resources? I am grateful to my librarian colleague Carol Reekie for a helpful section on this. And then what about the seminar group that is so common in master's courses – how do you join in in a seminar group effectively, without being either a shrinking violet on the one hand or dominating to the annoyance of your colleagues on the other? Seminar groups can be especially difficult to negotiate, especially if English is not your first language. And how do you present a paper well in a group? Finally, in Chapter 3, Esther Shreeve looks at some issues pertinent to students with specific learning difficulties.

Chapter 4 is about understanding the complex relationship between theory and practice. This is a relevant question for all who study theology, but this chapter will perhaps be of most help to those whose course demands some form of 'reflective practice' or reflection on practice. This may be in a placement or by the requirement to draw on present and past pastoral practice for assignments or by an expectation that you will engage your own story and identity in the theology you are studying. It is about being a reflective practitioner and about being able to be self-reflective.

Chapter 5 is about being scholarly. Please don't be put off if this sounds too dry or too difficult. The chapter will address some important basic issues about good academic practice – avoiding plagiarism, for example, and referencing work correctly. But beyond the technicalities we will look at how to use the language of the scholarly community, into which we enter when we do a postgraduate degree, without losing our own voice. This chapter should be of help to everyone, whether you are gladly embracing the scholarly community in hopeful anticipation of moving on to a doctorate or whether you are reluctantly putting a toe in the waters of 'academia' in order to enhance your practice and personal understanding.

Do you feel a little afraid of or even unhappy about the idea that you will need to bring a critical approach to matters of faith? Or do you warm to that possibility? Chapter 6 concerns the tension so many of us feel between suspicion and trust, between commitment and critique, when we reflect on our faith. It explores the issues that arise when we work ecumenically in an academic context and when we need to meet the critical expectations of higher education at the same time as remaining faithful to our tradition of faith.

Chapter 7 is especially for international students. The issues explored in Chapter 6 may be especially sharp for you. Then there are such different expectations of students in different countries: are you given set reading or expected to choose for yourself? Tested every week or not till the end of the year? Allowed to write freely on a topic or failed for not answering the question? What are the conventions for quoting authorities? Working in a language that is not your own affects how long it takes to read, how many words you need to do your assignment and how much you feel you can contribute to class discussion.

Finally, Chapter 8 addresses how to approach and to write a dissertation for a taught master's degree. It covers choosing a topic, finding a supervisor and how to design and execute an excellent dissertation from start to finish.

I hope you will find this book helpful. It will probably be most useful to you if you pick the chapters that cover the topics that most concern you, although reading it from cover to cover might bring all sorts of ideas to your attention that you might otherwise never have thought about. Most of all I hope you enjoy 'your MA in Theology' – that 'unique laboratory of sharing and exchange'.

The exquisite ivory book cover that is reproduced on the cover of this book depicts a great saint in many Christian traditions and the pope who sent missionaries to England, Gregory the Great (540–604). Committed to both the contemplative and the active life, he writes with the Holy Spirit on his shoulder.

# 1

# What Does it Mean to Study at Taught Master's Level?

Students on theology master's programmes come with all kinds of previous educational histories. This one has just completed an undergraduate degree in theology or religious studies; that one has a minimal background in theology but a PhD in astrophysics; a third one studied to be an RE teacher so long ago he doesn't like to remember. Then everyone has different professional and practical experience: from 20 years as an accountant to two years in parish ministry; from the young person who came to theological college last week and feels they have no pastoral experience, to the dentist at the local psychiatric hospital and the grandmother whose last adventure was to learn to fly and who celebrated her eightieth birthday in the first semester of the course. When I started my own postgraduate work in 1988, I had spent the last 14 years at home as a vicar's wife and bringing up three daughters; the young man sitting next to me in my first lecture looked very young and frighteningly academic.

You may feel most nervous and at a disadvantage if it has been a long time since you studied, but others have their hurdles to over-come too. Those who have written brilliant essays at undergraduate level may find it hard to engage with the reflective and practice-orientated requirements of many master's degrees in practical, pastoral, applied or contextual theology. It's hard to be awarded

45 when you are used to achieving 70. Then others may feel disadvantaged by being in a minority tradition. I will say more about these issues in Chapters 4 and 6, but here I mention my student who regarded the set assignment on our core module as 'frustratingly unsporting' (Bennett and Porumb, 2011, p. 43), because it expected a type of pastoral experience to which he as an Orthodox lay Christian felt he had had no access. If you feel you might not make the grade, you can be sure others are feeling the same.

# Master's level

How do we define what it means to work at 'master's' level? The very term is antiquated and masculine. Its origin is in the universities of medieval Europe, where Master, along with other titles like Scholar, Professor or Doctor, indicated how long you had studied, what if any teaching responsibilities you held and where you should walk in university processions – wearing what kind of academic dress. You became a 'Master' after you had been a 'Bachelor'.

Master's degrees today are earned in various ways. If you are reading this book, I expect you are earning yours by undertaking a one- or two-year course, full- or part-time, at some point subsequent to having taken a Bachelor's degree or having an equivalent qualification or equivalent experience. In many universities in Scotland, however, a master's is awarded as a first degree, and the universities of Cambridge and Oxford and Trinity College, Dublin award graduates master's degrees after a period of time, but these are not academic qualifications as such.

The Quality Assurance Agency for Higher Education (QAA), which produces frameworks for higher education qualifications in England, Wales and Northern Ireland, and separately for Scotland, publishes on the web a document outlining master's degree characteristics (QAA, 2010). This is a good place to start in asking what it means to work at master's level as most universities in the UK take their level descriptors and their assessment criteria from here.

Graduates of specialized/advanced study master's degrees typically have:

i)  subject-specific attributes
   • an in-depth knowledge and understanding of the discipline informed by current scholarship and research, including a critical awareness of current issues and developments in the subject
   • the ability to complete a research project in the subject, which may include a critical review of existing literature or other scholarly outputs.

ii) generic attributes (including skills relevant to an employment-setting)
   A range of generic abilities and skills that include the ability to:
   • use initiative and take responsibility
   • solve problems in creative and innovative ways
   • make decisions in challenging situations
   • continue to learn independently and to develop professionally
   • communicate effectively, with colleagues and a wider audience, in a variety of media. (QAA, 2010, pp. 13–14)

Master's degrees are awarded to students who have demonstrated:

- a systematic understanding of knowledge and a critical awareness of current problems and/or new insights, much of which is at, or informed by, the forefront of their academic discipline, field of study or area of professional practice
- a comprehensive understanding of techniques applicable to their own research or advanced scholarship
- originality in the application of knowledge, together with a practical understanding of how established techniques of research and enquiry are used to create and interpret knowledge in the discipline
- conceptual understanding that enables the student:
  - to evaluate critically current research and advanced scholarship in the discipline
  - to evaluate methodologies and develop critiques of them and, where appropriate, to propose new hypotheses.

Typically, holders of the qualification will be able to:

- deal with complex issues both systematically and creatively, make sound judgements in the absence of complete data, and communicate their conclusions clearly to specialist and non-specialist audiences
- demonstrate self-direction and originality in tackling and solving problems, and act autonomously in planning and implementing tasks at a professional or equivalent level
- continue to advance their knowledge and understanding, and to develop new skills to a high level.

And holders will have:

- the qualities and transferable skills necessary for employment requiring:
  - the exercise of initiative and personal responsibility
  - decision-making in complex and unpredictable situations
  - the independent learning ability required for continuing professional development. (QAA, 2010, p. 16)

This is quite daunting so I will pick out the key areas on which you should focus. All of these areas will be treated in more depth later in this book – this is a preliminary sketch of the territory.

## Independence

As a master's student, you will need to work independently. This is related to the question explored below of what it means to study on a 'taught' masters. You are expected to take initiative and responsibility, to plan your own studies and to think for yourself. 'You are your own boss', a student of mine said recently. As the criteria above make plain, this is related to the connections between master's studies and professional work. You may be taking a master's degree as a preparation for employment or as preparation for a doctoral degree, or you may be taking it as continuing professional development. A small number of people take master's degrees in theology just for the fun of it or for personal spiritual or intellectual development, but for most of us the academic work is connected to present or future practice, whether that is paid or voluntary, academic or professional. So it is not surprising that independence of thinking and working, self-direction, decision-making and problem-solving feature in the QAA criteria. These skills may be second nature to you after years of professional practice (and for these purposes I counted my 14 years bringing up my daughters very much as 'professional practice'). It is important to remember that we bring transferable skills *into* a master's degree as well as taking them *from* a master's degree.

On the other hand, this independence may be unnerving. You may have come straight from a highly directed undergraduate degree; you may have arrived from a country and an educational system that gives precise directions about what to read and tests you regularly in this. Whoever you are, you may feel that you are at sea in academia, that your thoughts are not worth much compared with those of your teachers and the writers you engage with, and that you have minimal skills in planning your academic work. I hope this book will help you, but nothing will help you as much as the painful step-by-step taking of risks and trying things out. We learn by doing, by acting, by making mistakes: *solvitur ambulando* –'it is solved by walking' – as Diogenes the Cynic said. The best master's students are those who have the courage to try something out independently, even if they get it wrong, and to learn from their mistakes.

# Critical engagement with current scholarship

The QAA criteria emphasize two aspects of engagement with published work in your field of study – first that it be current and second that it be critical. Gone are the days when you could get away with setting out only the classic positions on your topic, however worthily and excitingly they were laid out in the 1940s or the 1960s in books that appear on all undergraduate bibliographies. Master's study means finding out what the latest word on a subject is; what the current state of the argument and debate is. You should aim to have several serious items on your reference list published in the last five years. You do not, of course, have to agree with the 'latest word' – this is not about being trendy but about showing that you are working 'at the forefront of [your] academic discipline'. In our doctoral programme we call this having a conversation with 'key voices' in the subject area.

But 'current' is not enough; critical is also vital. The word 'critical' comes from the word for judgement – being critical is about being willing to exercise your own judgement. There is an element of this which is about your 'disposition' – about having enough confidence and trusting your own voice (about which there is more in Chapters 2 and 5) – but there is an element that can be learned through techniques.

Think of the matter as attempting to find a 'critical space'. Archimedes said, 'give me a place to stand on and I will move the world'. He was referring to the principle of leverage, but what he said is a good image for much more than physical leverage. To get a critical purchase we need to stand back. Please note that this is *not* the same as being 'objective' rather than 'subjective'. Making judgements is inevitably a subjective activity, but it is about finding a perspective from which we can see more than our immediate prejudices, learn more than we know already. John Ruskin described this as walking round and round the matter as if it were a polygon and seeing it from all angles. 'Mostly, matters of any consequence are three-sided, or four-sided, or polygonal; and the trotting round a polygon is severe work for people any way stiff in their opinions' (Ruskin, *Works* 16, p. 187). Here are some practical tips about how to do that 'trotting round a polygon', which may help in gaining a critical perspective.

- Take a historical perspective. Tell the story of how this view or practice came about, what it developed from, who advocated and who opposed it.
- Contextualize. Put the authors and the practices you are engaging with into their context. What period of time? What was going on politically or in other ways in the wider world at the time? What denomination is this material from? What part of the world is the author writing from?
- Make comparisons. How does this thinker compare with another? How does thinking in this period of time or in this ecclesial tradition compare with others?
- Allow theory and practice to critique each other. How does what a certain thinker or writer say match up to what you have experienced or what you know from your practice? Conversely and equally importantly, how does this thinker or writer offer a helpful critique, perhaps even an uncomfortable critique, to your practice and to the way you have understood your experience? The more uncomfortable you are the more you will learn.

Systematic attention to such a disciplined way of framing your work yields dividends. It is not a matter of pulling yourself up by your own bootlaces to become 'critical' or about being negative. The matter needs to be demystified – it concerns some quite specific moves that all of us can make.

## Being reflective

The skill of being reflective about your work and your approach to it is important at master's level. This skill lies behind the possibility of fulfilling some of the QAA's expectations – of critical awareness and critical evaluation, of the interpretation of knowledge and of the demonstration of originality. As with being critical, skills of being reflective can be developed in a disciplined way by attention to some very specific matters. You might ask yourself:

- Why did I choose this method, this author to engage with, this way of looking at things?
- Would I choose differently in retrospect? Why?
- Why did I *not* choose other methods or interpretations?
- How well did the methods and models I used work in practice to help me understand my material?
- Do I bring prejudgements and prior commitments to my work, and if so, what are these? How have they been challenged by what I have read or researched?

Always, always, ask the question 'Why?'

The best research is that which disconfirms what you thought when you started; the most fruitful essay that which makes you change your mind about something or see things differently. Otherwise, what have you learned?

## Communication

To quote John Ruskin again, 'The greatest thing a human soul ever does in this world is to see something, and tell what it saw in a plain way' (*Works* 5, p. 333). Or in the QAA's more prosaic words:

'Graduates of specialized/advanced study master's degrees typic-ally have … [a] range of generic abilities and skills that include the ability to … communicate effectively, with colleagues and a wider audience, in a variety of media.'

Effective communication in a theology master's may be in written words, in the spoken word in a presentation, in action in a placement or indeed in some other medium such as art or music. All these will be treated at various points throughout this book. I shall never deviate from emphasizing the need to be clear and plain. Clear communication means clear thinking. There is no better way to find out whether you understand something than to try and articulate it to someone else. Try it with an imaginary audience, if you haven't got a willing real one, and maybe have a recording device.

## A postscript

It is normal for universities to set out their assessment criteria publicly at all levels of study. It is wise to look at what is expected at master's level on your course, normally available in a module or course guide; to aim to fulfil what is required; and to expect a mark and feedback that reflect how well you have achieved this and comment on any ways you could have achieved it better.

## A 'taught' master's?

I have a picture in my room at work, drawn many years ago by my daughter. It is copied from a Spot cartoon and says under the three drawings: 'I taught Spot to whistle.' 'I can't hear him whistling.'

'I said I taught him; I didn't say he'd learned it.' I asked her to copy me this cartoon when the penny suddenly dropped for me that what mattered was what people learned not what people taught.

Once you become a postgraduate student, it is all about your learning. Of course, it is all about our learning from babyhood, but the educational system in the UK expects a big jump from undergraduate to master's procedures in learning. For a start, certainly in a theology master's, you are likely to be in a seminar group, with the expectation that you bring the reading and the reflection you have done between classes and share it. You will be asked to do seminar presentations and perhaps book reviews, and you will receive only a limited amount of information via lectures. You will have a huge amount of 'student-managed learning time' compared to 'classroom' time. And you will have to do library and internet searches for material. All this will be true whether you are on a face-to-face or a distance-learning course, although some practicalities may differ.

I have known many students for whom this is disconcerting – 'this is advertised as a "taught" course', they say, 'I expected more teaching'. So, what *can* you expect from the 'teachers' of such courses?

The teacher is acting as a kind of midwife to you. She is concerned for the healthy growth of this 'baby' in you, which is formed of all the understanding and skills and attitudes you develop and deploy on the course and eventually comes into the world in the shape of the assignments you present for assessment. So you can expect two major areas of help: the first is guidance and encouragement in developing the healthiest baby possible; the second is support and some detailed instructions in the struggle of giving birth.

So in respect of the first of these you may expect guidance by way of a 'module guide' or equivalent, in hard copy or on your institution's VLE (virtual learning environment). This spells out what you can expect to happen in each element of the course – practicalities of teaching, of assessment, of resources available, of expectations on you and deadlines you must meet. You can expect a warm and helpful engagement with where you are coming from and what your learning needs are. You can expect guidance on reading, but not to be spoon-fed with every reference you need – master's students are expected to do their own searches on catalogues and databases of the library and to find other resources, though you may indeed expect training to be offered on how to do this. You can expect timely feedback on any formative assessments you undertake, in order that you take comments into account for the final summative assessment.[1] On face-to-face courses actual class teaching will form only a small part of this guidance and encouragement (typically 25 hours class teaching to 225 hours student-managed learning), but it is a vital part and missed at your peril.

As for the struggle, the agony and the ecstasy, of giving birth to your summative assignments, you can expect some specific help. As well as guidance and assessment criteria set out in module guides, most courses would also expect to offer a student some form of personal or small-group help in preparing for an assignment. Do take note of what help is on offer and take advantage of it. And do so in time to make a difference to what you produce. Years of experience have taught me that students can raise their game – and raise their mark, significantly – by doing this.

There are four areas in which it is wise to seek advice:

---

1 A 'formative' assessment is a piece of work that does not count towards your final mark but enables you to develop through the feedback; a 'summative' assessment is one where the mark is part of your grade for the module.

- Am I writing to a good title? Sometimes titles for essays or other work are set; at other times the students are invited to work in an area that interests them, and the formation of a title question is part of the independent thinking required. Do take advice and guidance on this; your tutor/class teacher will have a good eye for what titles invite work at master's level and cover an appropriate amount of ground.
- Does my work-plan cover the right areas? This is an easy but vital stage to seek advice. Always plan what you are going to cover and how, and seek advice whether you have covered the right things.
- Are there any obvious resources I have missed out? Ask your tutor/class teacher to look at a list of key literature and resources you have produced and check whether anything glaringly obvious has been missed. She may also check whether your literature and resources are at the right level and whether they are up to date.
- Am I writing in the right style? Especially if you are a returner to study or English is not your first language, you may want to run a short section of your work past your tutor/class teacher to get some feedback.

Two things not to say to your tutor/class teacher:

- I really haven't thought through what I might do; I've just come so you can work this out for me.
- Please could you read these 15,000 words I have written and tell me what to miss out so I can get it down to 6,000 words?

These are your tasks not hers.

## Summing up

You may well feel apprehensive when starting a master's course. I have tried to demystify some of the vague expectations and fears you might have and to let you know you are not alone. Focusing on the QAA expectations, which are adopted and adapted by most universities, I have identified four areas to which you need to pay attention: working independently; critical engagement with current scholarship; being reflective and reflexive; and communication skills. Finally, I have looked at the meaning commonly given to the word 'taught' in a taught master's degree and attempted to suggest ways you could negotiate getting the best out of the teaching you receive.

# 2

# Core Study Skills for Master's Students 1

This and the following chapter deal with some core skills you will need to complete your master's degree well. I begin in this chapter with reflection and writing.

I have not put reading first because reading is not where we start. We start with who we are, with what we are bringing to the course by way of prior information and prior beliefs and commitments. This is true even if we are given reading to do before the course begins. Who is doing the reading? Where are we starting from? What are our questions and experiences, prejudices and desires, fears and expectations? All these will colour how and what we learn. To look at them closely and critically will enable us to learn effectively and fruitfully. So we start with reflection and writing. Writing things down is a way of thinking them through – I encourage you to write a reflective piece on where you are starting from, what your theological commitments are, what questions you are bringing and what you hope to learn, before you ever read anything or attend any class. Just for you.

Writing is also a key way we take charge of the process of our own learning. We are not just passive receptacles of others' ideas and of information overload, but we are the ones doing the learning, we are active subjects. So start writing on day one. Writing and reflection will stay with us each day and each week as we go through the course, and the assessed piece of writing at the end will be so much easier if we have been writing all along.

Chapter 3 will tackle reading, using the library, seminar skills and specific learning difficulties.

# Reflection

The quality of the content of everything we write or say or otherwise produce in master's work is dependent on the quality of our reflection. If you are doing an MA in some form of practical theology, then 'action/reflection' models will comprise a core element of the method by which you go about your work.[1] But reflection is not the prerogative of practical theology, it is a constituent element of all serious theological work, indeed of cognitive and creative work in all fields.

The basic model I am working with here is that we take in 'stuff' – from listening, from reading, from experience – and we reflect on it. I could say, 'we think about it', which would be true, but I prefer the term 'reflect' as it implies a certain attention, a stillness and a taking of time; a reciprocity between what we bring and what we receive; a looking at things from different angles. We have to do the processing before we can produce something in the public realm that makes sense to others and makes a contribution to the subject, whether that something be an essay, a seminar presentation, a verbatim report or an artefact.

In order to reflect we must see something well. John Ruskin, the nineteenth-century art and social critic to whom I have already referred in Chapter 1, said that 'To see clearly is poetry, prophecy,

---

1 See Chapter 4.

and religion, – all in one' (*Works* 5, p. 333).[2] This takes time and demands attention to what is new to us, rather than a quick jumping to conclusions or hurrying on so fast we miss things. A former colleague of mine, Brother Patrick Moore, used to say, 'teaching is the overflow of contemplation'. So is good work for a master's degree.

Contemplation or prayer may be for some a profound way of reflecting. Karl Barth said that, 'The first and basic theological work is *prayer*' (1963, p. 160; emphasis in original). He writes of theological work happening in a realm that not only has windows outwards to the surrounding world but 'also and above all has a skylight' (p. 161). Likewise, for the Orthodox tradition, theology itself is *theoria* – a good 'seeing' that goes hand in hand with prayer. Prayer and contemplation are ways proper attention may be given to all aspects of a situation and we may hold openness – to what is outside of us, within us and currently beyond us (Leach, 2007; Moore, 2003; Soskice, 2007).

When conducting study skills classes for master's students I often brainstorm with the group – 'If you had an hour in which to "reflect", what would you do?' The answers are revealing. Some people talk of different ways in which the brain and heart can be stilled and relaxed in order to allow space for attention – walking the dog, listening to music, having a bath. Other answers indicate the importance of allowing the creative 'right brain' to get a look in – painting or drawing, writing a poem, making a picture or mind map. The act of writing itself as a way of reflecting is important, perhaps through keeping a journal, writing notes on reading or on some experience. For many people, reflection is connected with trying to articulate what it is they know or are struggling to

---

2 For further development of the theme of seeing well in relation to theology, see Zoë Bennett, 2013, *Using the Bible in Practical Theology: Historical and Contemporary Perspectives*, Aldershot: Ashgate, chapters 6–8.

understand. In this, writing may help, but so might speaking out loud to oneself or speaking with others in conversation. A brainstorm itself is a type of corporate reflection. Reflection back from others – of understanding or of question and challenge – enables our own further and deeper reflection.

# Writing

## The influence of history

How you write will be determined by your past history of writing. Take a moment to stop reading this book and reflect. Write down the following:

- What was my most enjoyable experience ever of writing?
- What was my most successful experience ever of writing?
- What was my most painful experience associated with writing?
- How do I feel about writing?

Karen's most enjoyable experiences of writing were twofold. She remembered, aged about nine, writing creative descriptions in school – of nature mainly. Then she also deeply enjoyed writing letters to her mother, who wrote her wonderful letters back. Not surprisingly these were also her most successful attempts at writing – she got great comments from her teacher on the school essays, and her mother clearly loved her letters. Her most painful experiences came much later, sitting at the computer trying to write academically and feeling it always came out in a too dense and rather constipated way – good enough but dull and difficult. 'If only you could write like you teach', said people who read it; 'If only I could write like I used to write to my mother', she thought. Gradually she began to work out what was wrong. She was always afraid her academic writing wasn't good enough, looking over her shoulder at those who might judge it, her 'superiors'. Everything had to be crammed in; everything had to be perfect. (Some people call this your 'internal editor'.) She got over it quite dramatically, one Sunday afternoon between 5 p.m. and 8 p.m., sitting by the fire in the house on her own with a laptop and just writing – nonstop, no references yet, about something she knew well and loved and, above all, for herself – 'I can chuck this out if it's no good'. But she didn't chuck it out – she published it. And the writing coach at university, who had put red ink all over her last piece, sat there reading and reading, entranced, then turned round and asked 'What happened?'

You will have guessed that 'Karen' is me. Your story will be different. You may have verbal diarrhoea, not constipation, in which case the remedy will be different. But my central point is that without attention to what gives us energy and what blocks us, we will get nowhere. Writing demands attention to psychology as well as to technique. Attention to your own writing history will enable you to unearth wellsprings of creativity by rejoicing in and working with those aspects of writing that have given you pleasure and a sense of achievement. It will also identify for you where there are likely to be blocks and fears, which you might like to address by talking them through with a friend or a tutor or by using books like Gillie Bolton's or Jennifer Moon's to do some self-help (Bolton, 2010; Moon, 2006).

## The style you bring with you

You come into your master's programme with some styles of writing already at your fingertips. The trick is to identify what they are – to use their strengths and avoid their weaknesses. What kinds of writing do you do most? Reports? Sermons? Poetry? Texts? Emails? Essays?

If you have come straight from an undergraduate degree you will be used to writing essays; the task will be to identify what characterizes a master's essay over an undergraduate one (see Chapter 1). Or perhaps, if you are working in some form of reflective or practical theology for the first time, it will be to learn how to write appropriately in the first person. The temptation will be to repeat a well-worn style and all your old mistakes without venturing into something more bold and mature. On the other hand, the great advantage you have is knowing how an essay is formed and shaped and being familiar with a basic academic feel to writing.

Those who write reports at work will have the invaluable skill of being precise and to the point and of keeping things in order. But there are two things you will do well that you need to keep in check when writing an academic essay. The first is to list salient points in a bullet-point list. If you are a skilled report writer, my advice to you is to impose a self-discipline of using no bullet points at all for the whole first year of your master's. Bullet-point lists are too superficial. They encourage you to drop an idea in and move on, whereas in an academic piece of work you are invited to stay with an idea and to develop it discursively, taking a good look before moving on. Never quote a list of bullet points from another author – that compounds the problem as you are not only dropping in ideas without discussion but dropping in ideas that are not your own without discussion. The second problem experienced report writers encounter is a tendency to keep the main ideas and conclusions till the final paragraph of the essay, in the manner of a report. In an academic essay you should be building up the thesis and discussing it from page 1, and the conclusion at the end should simply sum up what you have been explicitly developing and arguing for all along.

The sermon writer can be spotted a mile away. He is passionate about his material – a great gift in writing. He knows how to develop a theme from many angles – also an advantage in essay writing. But he preaches at the reader. His work is littered with the words 'we need to' and 'we must'. Who is 'we', and why do 'we' 'need to', why 'must' we? If you are used to writing sermons it is all too easy to assume some sort of Christian audience who need exhortation and who do not need evidence or argument. Banish the words 'we', 'need' and 'must', and that simple technique will help you get out of sermon mode.

The text and email writer may be sloppy in spelling, punctuation and grammar and boringly simple in style or unable to develop beyond the pragmatic bare bones of an issue. On the other hand, the blog writer, as in a different way the poet, may have skills of laying out deep thoughts, musing on them creatively, engaging the personal in words that catch the attention and imagination of the reader.

The crucial thing is that you think through what you are bringing with you, how it might help you and how it might hinder you.

## Writing a journal

Keeping a journal throughout your master's could transform your learning and work. Start straight away. The journal may be used to record or explore your feelings, record facts and explore their implications, note what you have learned from class, from reading, from your daily work, from conversations or from reflection. Keep it daily if you can. Use a hand-written notebook, keep files on your computer or use whatever means you like.

Apart from the obvious but overlooked fact that such a journal will store a mass of information invaluable in the writing of assignments, the actual writing of it helps in myriad ways. If you think it will take too long, try Gillie Bolton's six-minute writing exercise and see how much you can write in a very short time (Bolton, 2010, pp. 107–9). Just set yourself a title, set a stop-watch for six minutes and start writing. Do not stop, do not lift pen from paper or fingers from keyboard for the six minutes, whatever nonsense you write. Even if you just did this every day, with the title, 'What have I learned today?', the results would be a treasure.

Writing daily helps you find and trust your own voice and your own writing style. It helps you develop your own thinking and articulate how it is developing. You don't have to show it to anyone!

## Writing an essay

The philosopher Plato used a picture of the human being as a charioteer driving a chariot pulled by two horses. He said Reason is the Charioteer, Spirit and Desire the two unruly horses, often pulling in different directions. Adapting this image gives a powerful picture of what it is like writing an essay. In writing we need to harness the two horses of our passion and of our rhetorical style. They are there in us, a passion and a style of writing, but in a raw state they may be all over the place and lead us a merry dance, even wreck our chariot/essay. At the same time, paradoxical as this may sound, they are actually often subdued and hidden, and we are hardly using any of their force. So think of writing an essay as discovering the force of passion and of good style and harnessing these to work together to get our writing to go where we want it to go and to achieve what we want it to achieve.

'Don't get it right, get it written.' This is the best tip I can give you. We all have an internal editor who sits on our shoulders and whispers, 'You're missing something out'; 'You haven't read enough'; 'That sentence doesn't make sense'; 'You really don't know what your argument is.' Please don't get me wrong: it is important to include relevant material, enriching to read enough, vital to have sentences that make sense, and without an argument we don't have an essay. But – and it is a crucial 'but' – these things come in partnership with the act of writing not before it. As we write we develop our argument; when we review our writing in an ongoing way we see where we need to read more to help our argument and where there are gaps. When we do the final editing, we note and change sentences that don't make sense, and we correct spelling and grammar.

## Finding a style

The style in which you write is a matter of great importance. Balancing what we want to do and what works well is always a problem, as in the well-known limerick:

> There was a young girl from Japan
> Who wrote verses that never would scan.
> When told that the thing
> Ought to go with a swing,
> She said, 'Yes, but I always try to get as many words into the last line as I can'.

There are two fundamental principles, which take us back to the analogy of the charioteer and the two horses. The first is that your style should be your own, reflecting your character, your engagement with the material, above all your passion for what you are writing. It should draw on all your own strengths and not be a mimicry of someone else's way of writing. The second is that it should be clear and readable. To achieve this you need some technical skill. This is technical skill we can all learn – for example, not using unnecessary words or clichés and using short sentences. By far the best book I have ever read that helped me to write is William Zinsser's *On Writing Well* (2006), first published in 1976 and now in its 7th edition. Being clear does not inhibit your personality from coming through – it allows it to come through. Remember you are the charioteer, harnessing your views and feelings on the one hand and drawing on your technical skills on the other, to get your chariot where *you* want it to go.

I am regularly asked about the use of 'I' in an academic essay. There are no hard and fast rules, but here are some guidelines:

- Ask your tutor or supervisor what is expected on your programme.
- Avoid using 'we' when you mean 'I', as in this example, 'After considering Moltmann's work we will offer a critique of contemporary ideas about the social trinity.'
- Always use 'I' when describing your own practice in a pastoral theology essay.
- Avoid awkward uses of the third person such as 'The author of this essay believes'.

It is becoming increasingly frequent in all disciplines to use 'I'. This is partly for stylistic reasons – 'we' sounds pompous and unreal, and using the passive, 'it will be argued', is clunky. It is also because the academic community has increasingly recognized the importance of the knowing subject – that is, the person who actually does the knowing – in the construction of knowledge, so the use of 'I' is philosophically and epistemologically appropriate.

My deliberate use of 'epistemologically' raises another important issue of style. What is the place of long words and jargon? If you look up 'jargon' in a dictionary you will find that one of its definitions is negative and one positive. The negative one is 'convoluted, meaningless, pretentious and vague'. No one wants the essay they write or the essay they mark to be convoluted, meaningless, pretentious and vague. The positive definition refers to the common language of a profession or trade, the specialized or technical language of a group that becomes a common idiom in which they can communicate succinctly and with precision. To use language in this way in an academic essay is to convey meaning precisely but it is also, importantly, to show that you are familiar with the lexicon of those who work in your subject area. 'Understanding' is important here. To use technical words without understanding them is a disaster. You are not writing a sermon, you are not talking at the school gate, you are writing an academic essay – and in each case there is an appropriate language. So I used 'epistemologically' because it conveyed precisely what I meant – 'in relation to the science of how we currently understand the act of knowing' – more elegantly and in fewer words, and because I would expect that master's students in theology either know this word or will benefit by coming to know it. However, I would not, for example, use the word 'Phyletism' unless I were writing for Orthodox readers, in which case I would use it freely. What is needed is precise writing, where all words are fully understood by the writer, where the common lexicon of the subject is used well, with no convoluted expressions in pretentious long sentences using words with as many syllables as possible.

## Planning

I return again to the idea of the charioteer steering the horses. In order to get where you want to go you must *decide* where you want to go and by what route. Planning is a word that may cause panic. People vary from the constipated ones who cannot write a word until they have a good plan that covers every detail and all eventualities, to those afflicted by verbal diarrhoea who never plan at all. Neither of these ways of working is ideal. You need to work with your own strengths and temperament, not against them but tempering them and finding a place where you can plan enough to have control while leaving enough freedom to move and indeed confidence to start writing at all.

There are different ways of planning a piece of work. You will develop your own and probably have done so already before starting a master's degree, but here are some ideas to try out if you aren't satisfied with your current method. The classic essay plan consists of one to two sides of A4 paper detailing what topics you will cover, in what order, with a little indication of what chunks of your material will go where and perhaps also suggesting how many words you will use for each section. Allocating provisional word lengths is helpful in giving you an idea of how much detail you can go into and how much material you can include in each section; it can also help you not to write twice as many words as you are allowed and thus end up with the painful and time-consuming task of losing words.

Some people have a real problem with linking their ideas into an argument, which is a crucial skill for master's students. One method of planning that can help here is to write an abstract of about 200 words, explaining the content and argument of your essay. You will find abstracts at the head of most contemporary journal articles, so look at a few to get the idea. Here is an example:

This essay seeks to make a case for a particular historical method of doing practical theology and explores what such a method has to offer through the specific case of John Ruskin. It first develops the theme of Ruskin as a reader of texts – the aesthetic, the social and the scriptural – asking what different kinds of 'reading' may be involved and probing the epistemological assumptions of the kind of 'seeing' he commends and believes he is engaged in. It then considers the implications both of the multidisciplinarity implied by his methods and also of the role of the 'amateur' which is suggested. It then addresses the question of presentation; practical theologians need to consider how to present their theological reflection and interpretation in such a way that it effectively challenges public understanding and inspires public action, and here Ruskin can help us greatly. The essay concludes with some reflections on the hermeneutics of using a historical paradigm of this sort. (Bennett, 2011, p. 203)

It might not be possible to be so exact right at the beginning of a piece of work, but you do need to grasp early on two things that this abstract shows: what the key points will be that you will argue for and, crucially, how they will hang together and develop one from the other as your essay goes on.

Standing back from your material and getting this kind of clarity is difficult. You may find it easier to do pictorial, using a mind-map or possibly a Venn diagram, to order your thinking. Here, used with permission, is a Venn diagram one of my master's students developed to show the plan of her dissertation argument about pastoral care of women in leadership in the churches (see Figure 1). We can see immediately what her key and subsidiary points are and where they connect and what they build up to; that is the issue of flourishing in the middle.

## Figure 1 Planning and organizing your ideas

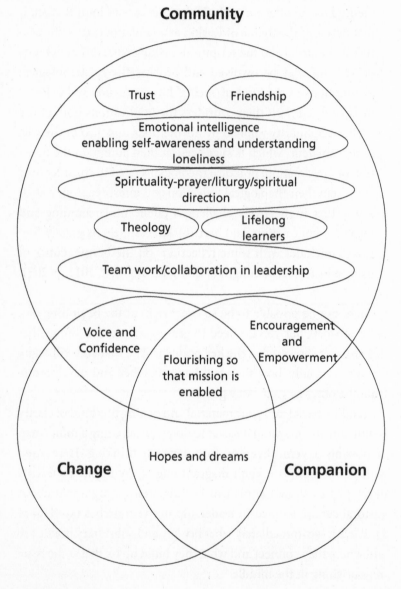

Rengert 2013, p. 43

On the other hand, there are those who are at their best when talking not writing. If this is you, use a recording device and try explaining briefly what the key argument of your work is. Imagine someone had asked you about it at a party – your answer has to be brief and interesting! Or if you are a teacher, imagine how you would talk in front of your class – clearly, succinctly and engaging interest. Because my besetting sin is to get bogged down in detail, I make myself talk my planning out loud while driving. For this method, you either need a recording device, a good memory or a layby in which to stop and write it down.

## Developing an argument

A good essay should be like a cross between an iceberg and an express train: an iceberg, because for the one eighth you see on the surface there are another seven eighths underneath; and an express train, because it starts somewhere and moves swiftly through its journey to its destination. Teasing out these images can tell us much about constructing an argument in an essay.

The express train has a starting station, a journey to travel and a destination station; an essay has an introduction, a series of sections, within which there are a series of paragraphs, and a conclusion. The introduction needs a departure board: 'Cambridge Station – this train is bound for Darlington via Peterborough, Newark and York.' At Peterborough, Newark and York there should be clear signposting of how far we have got and a sense that we have got here to York, because we came via Newark rather than via Manchester. We get to York via Newark (if we start in Cambridge) – it is a process of moving on via somewhere. By analogy, we get to later sections of an essay via the earlier ones, and the later ones should be explicitly built on the argument of the earlier ones. Look at your final sections and ask yourself: Can a reader see that

I could not have got here without my earlier sections? Am I clearly building the end on the beginning and the middle? At Darlington the passengers should be told to disembark because they have arrived and perhaps even told where they might get to if they took an onward train.

Paragraphs are a little like pieces of train track in this analogy. If they are too short they make for a bumpy and disjointed ride. Getting the paragraphs right – each one dealing with either a new point or a new development of a point and taking us a little further on – makes for good argument. They should never be used just to drop something in in a single sentence or two and then move on. The great Russian pianist Sviatoslav Richter played every phrase of his music with a consciousness of what part it was playing in the whole piece; just so every paragraph should have its place in the architecture of the whole essay. 'Among the most outstanding of Richter's characteristics was his uncanny ability to illuminate the minutest details while at the same time making them converge into a single unified whole' (Siepman, 1997, pp. 8–9).

And the iceberg? If you look back to Chapter 1 you will see that the expectations of master's graduates involve 'an in-depth knowledge and understanding of the discipline informed by current scholarship and research, including a critical awareness of current issues and developments in the subject', suggesting that master's students need a certain 'mastery' of their subject. Trying to squeeze everything you know into any given piece of work is impossible. What the work should display is an underlying grasp of the issues, gained by reflection and by reading, in which the tip of the iceberg gives away the seven eighths underneath. Chapter 5 will explore how this is done in more detail.

Two things your work definitely needs are argument and evidence. Your own argument should be the main voice in the text. What grounds can you give for the views you offer? What might be the counterarguments? Who else in the literature might support you or challenge you? How might practice or empirical evidence support or challenge you? Assertion of a viewpoint is insufficient without exploration, which involves making an argument and bringing in evidence.

## Editing

The internal editor is a demon while we are writing but an angel when we do the editing. Do leave long enough for the editing process – as long as you have for the writing is a good rule of thumb, shocking though that may sound to those who have left an hour or two to check undergraduate essays in the past. Think what you have to do.

- Read over the whole essay, preferably out loud, to see if it makes sense, and correct it where it doesn't. This may take a while as usually the things you have written in a way that does not make sense are the things you haven't understood well, so making them make sense requires an effort to understand them.
- Make use of the spellcheck on the computer – then check *beyond* the spellcheck for such witticisms as 'do unto otters as you would have them do unto you'.
- Make use of the grammar check on the computer and check for yourself as you read out loud.
- Check every single reference, first that it is done correctly according to the rules of your university, which will be readily available on the website; and second that you have included all page numbers where necessary, correctly. Your marker will probably be spot-checking these!
- Check for plagiarism. This is copying someone else's work without using quotation marks and/or without giving the reference

to where the quotation comes from. It is easy to do in these days of the internet, or if you were in a hurry, taking notes from a book. It is usually very easy for a marker to spot. It is an offence that results normally in a fail mark and sometimes in disciplinary action. If you are worried about doing this inadvertently, please do consult your tutor; most staff are more than happy to help and advise. Your university will have rules about plagiarism, which should be publicly available in the Academic Regulations and Module Guides. Furthermore, many universities offer or require that you put your work through some software (Turnitin) that detects plagiarism. If you have the opportunity to do this before handing in, it is well worth taking it.

- Ask someone else to read over your work and check for spelling, grammar and clarity.

## In summary

I have deliberately started with you as the reflecting and writing subject. I hope this chapter has given you a vision of three things: first, the priority of reflection and of your own thinking in the work that you do on your master's course; second, the significance of the passion you bring to the topics you engage with; and third, the importance of supporting that passion and directing it to do the work you want it to do in your assignments through sustained attention to skills and techniques.

# 3

# Core Study Skills for Master's Students 2

## with Carol Reekie and Esther Shreeve

This chapter looks at three rather different sets of core skills, and to write it I have drawn on the skills and expertise of my colleagues. The first issue addressed is reading. Reading is a vital way to inform and to challenge our writing and reflection and to widen our horizons. In order to read effectively we need to use our resources well, and that includes the library and e-resources available through it.

Next come seminar skills. The seminar is the environment in which so much learning on a master's course happens. It is one element in your tool kit as you wrestle with new discoveries. For some the regular meeting with others, face to face or via the internet, is the highlight of the course. For others it is a rather painful experience that needs to be carefully negotiated to get something out of it and to put something in.

Finally, this chapter addresses specific learning difficulties such as dyslexia, and offers targeted help and guidance and suggests resources to find further help.

# Reading

## Reading efficiently

So once you have got your books and articles, on paper or electronically, what will you do with them?

There are some things you cannot do. You are not reading purely for pleasure, so however fascinating Barth's work is, you do not have the ten years it has been calculated to take to read his entire output. You may not even have the whole day to read Marcella Althaus-Reid's *The Queer God*, which you have just discovered and is changing your life. On the other hand, you may decide this is worth a whole day; this is a borderline for master's students. Now you are concentrating in your studies on a smaller area than you did as an undergraduate, so you have time to go for depth as well as breadth. Furthermore, that depth will be expected of you. There are times when one author we read brings us to a totally new place in our thinking, and in a master's degree developing that thinking in conversation with that author gives us the chance to push ourselves and to display a real grasp of the subject matter.

Most of the time, however, the skill is to 'raid' a wide selection of material. The wide selection is necessary because of the need to understand the state of the question in current debate and to engage critically with it from various perspectives. You do not want a reference list that is too small or only has material from before 1980 or from one perspective, perhaps just Catholic or just Evangelical. The 'raiding' is necessary because you need to cover much in the time and, more importantly, you need to use a range of material to develop your own argument.

Some tips on the art of 'raiding': look at the contents list and the index of a book or the abstract of an article to see whether this work will help you and in what ways. In the case of a book, only read the sections you need. Read introductions and conclusions of articles and of chapters – these often give you the guts of the argument. Read as fast as you can – some people read down the middle of a page – skim till you come to what you need to engage with for your work and then go into the slow lane. I have another tip, which I have never seen anyone else advocate, so treat it with caution: read from the back of an article or a book or a chapter. This enables you to see where the author ends up and whether it is worth knowing how he or she got there. If it is, read back a little further.

The important thing at master's stage is always to use your secondary sources as a way of engaging with your own thinking. This is one reason why writing comes before reading. You need to know something of your own thinking, in quite a disciplined way, before you decide which 'conversation partners' – a good way of thinking of secondary authors – can help you develop that thinking. Of course, they will challenge your ideas with fresh material, which will expand your reflection and may even invite you to revise your opinions. It is always good to make clear in your work when this happens as it demonstrates your learning.

How much do you need to read? This is not the kind of solid school or undergraduate essay in which it was sufficient to summarize the key arguments of certain authors, showing how various points could be debated with argument and counterargument. This remains a basic skill but needs to be supplemented and built on. The range of authors needs to be wider, the choice more adventurous (*your* adventure not the tutor's – supplement the bibliography you are given in class with material you have found for yourself). Further, you need to engage what your authors are saying with your own views, your own practice and your own experience.

But you are not doing a doctorate (yet!). You do not need to read everything that has been said in this area and to have something original to say on top of that. You need to read enough to have a clear grasp of the subject. As the QAA puts it (see Chapter 1, p. 3),

> Graduates of specialized/advanced study master's degrees typically have … an in-depth knowledge and understanding of the discipline informed by current scholarship and research, including a critical awareness of current issues and developments in the subject.

There are two adjectives that should describe your reading and your use of that reading: critical and contextual. Reading work from different perspectives helps in being critical but it is also vital to ask yourself questions about the trustworthiness of the material you read, the soundness of its research methods and its scholarship and the coherence of its arguments. One area to think about that helps enormously in weighing up a work as you read it is to ask about the context it comes out of. When was it written? Where was it written (historical and geographical and cultural context)? Was it written out of a particular Christian or other tradition? Is the author ideologically committed to a viewpoint or an underlying stance, and if so is he or she aware of that? None of this is a problem in itself; being unaware of it in your use of material is a problem.

## Taking notes on reading

Taking notes on reading may be done in many different ways and serves a variety of functions. Looking at the functions can help in seeing what ways might be helpful.

There is information gathering. You may be gathering facts or you may be gathering useful quotations. In that case you need a tidy arrangement of where to keep this information. Will you put all information from one source in one place or will you group information according to subject matter? Whichever you chose, do not fail to note the book's or internet site's full reference details and the page number from which your information or quotation came! This will save hours casing in libraries or on the internet later. Do not forget also to put any words you write down verbatim, or copy and paste, into quotation marks *now* to avoid inadvertent plagiarism. You won't remember later. Will you keep all these notes on computer files or use index cards?

Notes do not only record and store information, they are an aid to you in thinking through what you read and in recording your thoughts for when you come back to the work. There are all kinds of ways of stimulating this reflection and recording it. One is to have a rule that when you have finished reading an article or a chapter of a book, you simply write down briefly your reactions to it and how it might be useful in your work. That will help you articulate a critical perspective and also help you sort out what is useful to this piece of work and what is fascinating but for another day.

There are more complex ways of keeping the notes you take in order and combining factual information and reflection. You could use Microsoft OneNote or other note-taking software. I have found that a simple table such as Figure 2 can be helpful in critical thinking about reading: you can use it for single items of reading or for multiple items.

You can see how this method allows you to record carefully where key ideas are in the literature at the same time as enabling you to reflect critically on the material. Furthermore, it focuses your attention on what you need from this material for *your argument* and moves you away from a purely descriptive dumping into your essay 'everything that Gorringe says in this useful book'.

## Figure 2 Making Notes

| Reference | Key point | Importance to work | Reflection |
|---|---|---|---|
| T. J. Gorringe, *Furthering Humanity: A Theology of Culture*, Aldershot: Ashgate, 2004, p. 1 | Definition of human culture based on Geertz's image of 'animals suspended in webs of significance' | I will need to define culture if I am going to make it a key point in my essay | This particular definition makes good sense to me and strengthens the idea I am working with of human beings making meaning out of their world. I will have to see whether there are competing definitions of culture |
| Ditto, chapter 1 pp. 12–16 | Critique of Richard Niebuhr's 'Christ and culture' typology as insufficiently nuanced and too dependent on high culture | I was thinking of using Niebuhr's typology but now realize I can only do so if I address Gorringe's criticisms | May not use Niebuhr. Gorringe has made me realize that at any given time: a) we do not live in one 'culture' but in cross-currents of many 'cultures'; and b) that a Christian may be negative towards one element and positive towards another element of the culture(s) that affect them. |

# Using the library – Carol Reekie

Before you can read you have to find what you are going to read. I am grateful to my colleague Carol Reekie, Librarian of the Cambridge Theological Federation, for contributing this section on using the library.

The aim of this section is to provide you with a number of ways of acquiring the information you need for your assignments and dissertation. The main focus will be on how to access electronic resources rather than the more traditional printed works, as libraries are now able to offer the library user a choice of format in which to view the required information. With the advent of the internet, finding information has never been easier, or has it? Although the internet has made access to millions of articles and items possible, it has also produced information overload. These next few pages will help you to find your way through the mass of information and make the best use of your available time.

Finding the right resources for your assignment or your dissertation can be very daunting at first glance. There is a great temptation to opt for the first items you find, particularly if you are under time constraints. If you are pursuing an MA by distance learning or part-time study, you may not have easy access to your institution's library. Even if you are on site, you should first check the library pages on the institution's website to see what is available and if there are any useful links to resources. Library webpages can vary considerably from a few lines to a very extensive listing of all the resources in your subject area. If this is not possible, a visit to the library is a must. Before you embark upon your studies it is important to find out what is available. If you are a part-time student or a distance learner, you can save a great deal of time by undertaking all the catalogue and webpage searching away from the library. This will enable you to make the most efficient use of your time in the library.

Don't just limit yourself to books and peer-reviewed journals. Other potential sources include: dissertations, conference proceedings, bibliographical references, newspapers, government publications, databases, organization reports, encyclopaedias, web resources as well as social media such as blog posts and podcasts. The library staff will be able to advise you on how to obtain access to these types of resources.

In order to find the information that you require, you need to select the appropriate search tools. Here are some tips that you may find useful.

## Books

Books are a useful starting point as they provide an overview of a subject. Look at the library catalogue. What resources can you find in your areas of interest? Is the catalogue easy to use? If you have not had any training in the use of the library catalogue, ask the librarian to show you how to use it or check to see if there are any leaflets or videos available.

Many people are familiar with keyword searching on Google and expect a library catalogue to search in the same way. This is not always the case. Some catalogues have a completely different interface and offer both a quick search and advanced search facility. Other catalogues use 'Boolean' operators rather than keywords. This greatly reduces the number of results displayed. It simply involves adding the word 'AND' to two keywords. For example, to search for Colin Gunton – Christian Faith, use Gunton AND Faith. The words 'NOT' and 'OR' can be used in the same way.

Truncation is also used in some catalogues and databases. This involves using an asterisk (*) at the beginning or end of a word and allows you to search for a number of words during a single search. For example, libr* will bring up items that contain the word 'library', 'libraries', 'librarian' and 'librarianship'. Check to see what search method is compatible with your institution's library catalogue.

Once you have located the books you require on the catalogue, ensure that you write down the classification number, the filing system by which you can find the book and the location. This will save a lot of time as your library might have several different collections housed in various locations other than the main library. If the library does not own a particular work that you require it may purchase a copy or try to obtain it through the inter-library loan service. This is usually a nationwide service whereby colleges or universities agree to loan their stock to other institutions. Not all colleges participate in this scheme, so it is important to discuss your needs with the library staff as there may be informal ways of obtaining the resources that you require.

Many libraries also offer electronic books, known as e-books. These can be extremely useful, particularly if you cannot visit the library in person or need to check some basic information quickly. Some libraries have individual e-books while others may have a subscription package. Check to see if your institution subscribes to any e-books that might be of use. It is worth attending a training session, if available, or obtaining a leaflet on how to use e-books. If you need a username and password to access a subscription package, make sure you receive the necessary details early on in the academic year.

## Journals

Journals and conference proceedings provide the most current thinking in your specific field of study, so are worth investigating. Once you have embarked upon your MA, check to see what journals your institutional library provides. Is there a list? Does it offer both printed and electronic versions? If it has individual electronic journal subscriptions, what are the usernames and passwords? Is there a generic username and password for all the subscriptions? Obtaining the usernames and passwords is particularly important if you want to search the electronic journals when off-site.

Gone are the days when you had to trawl through journal indexes to find useful articles. There are now a number of databases that will do the work for you. It is important to check to see if the library subscribes to any of these journal databases. If so, what journals are included? How easy is it to use? Is training provided? Are there any helpful leaflets or videos available? Check to see how far back the electronic archive goes. Some journal titles have only the last five years digitized, others may have a far longer back run. Does the database provide full text access or just abstracts? It is important to note if the journal you are interested in has full text coverage. Some titles have a 12-month delay before an issue is digitized, so you will have to consult the printed version of the journal if this is the case.

Journals are often an underused resource, even though they provide current information. As with books, look at the listed citations. Where has the author drawn information from? Can any other interesting articles be identified? Equally, journals can provide a historical view on a given topic and enable the development of particular ideas to be traced.

## Databases

There are a number of general databases that include a variety of published formats. These can be useful as they bring to your attention resources that you may be unaware of. Unfortunately each database is different as there is no standard format. Some are easier to use than others, so mastering one does not guarantee mastering others, which may not be organized the same way. The temptation is to become familiar with just one and ignore the rest. This is potentially to miss out on some useful information, so it is worth persevering and mastering a couple. Many databases allow you to save your searches in a folder that is accessible from wherever you are in the world. This avoids the need to download everything. Some databases will even provide the citations of the articles you have saved in your preferred citation style – Harvard, for example.

## Internet

For many the expectation is that everything can be found on the internet. Although this may be true to some extent, there is so much information available that finding exactly what you require can be time consuming. It is therefore important to give yourself plenty of time to do this. Thinking of good keywords will reduce the number of results that are displayed. The more specific the term the more relevant the results will be.

There are a number of search engines available that will help you navigate your way around the internet. They each have their strengths and weaknesses, and the way they search for inform-ation can differ considerably, so you may want to try different ones. For example, if you are searching using the terms 'children's spirituality', you will find that the number of results and the order of their rankings will differ in each search engine. This is because some only index the keywords from the title while others index the keywords from the whole entry. The number of search results can also differ. For example, a search for 'pastoral care' on Bing brought up three million items, while Google provided eight million and Google Scholar 400,000. Some websites have a limited lifespan, so ensure you record the URL and access date.

The internet provides access to many types of information, so it is important to evaluate it and not be too trusting. Don't just judge it against other items on the web – you need to assess its relevance, quality and authority. Some things to consider are:

- Is it relevant?
- Who is the author?
- Who is it published by? Is it an authoritative source? For example, peer-reviewed journals are more authoritative than journals that are not.
- How current is it?
- Is it biased? What is the point of view?
- Is it accurate?
- Why was it written? What audience is it aimed at?
- How detailed and in-depth is it?
- Is it consistent?
- Does the item contain any notes or a bibliography?

There is a huge amount of information available, and the internet is a great resource, but as with books and journals you must always cite your sources. Do not be tempted just to cut and paste – cite your source, which will demonstrate your breadth of knowledge and help you compile a bibliography.

And finally, it is very important to organize the downloaded resources in such a way that they are easily retrievable. Using folders to organize computer-stored data is recommended. Organize emails and attachments, spreadsheets and written work. And always back everything up.

## Other libraries

When embarking on a course, you do not have to limit yourself to your institution's library. Public libraries are often a good source of information. Many universities are members of SCONUL (Society of College, National and University Libraries) and as such are able to offer access to their libraries to students from other institutions. This can be particularly useful for part-time or distance-learning students, as it allows the borrowing of books and journals from libraries of institutions local to the user. The scheme covers most of the universities in the UK and Ireland (www.sconul.ac.uk). Check to see if your library is a member. If you are using a number of different libraries, it is a good idea to keep a record of where the resources used are from. This will enable you to locate an item quickly when compiling a bibliography.

## Seminar skills

Most theology master's programmes that are taught in face-to-face classes are based around seminar groups. If you are a distance learner it is likely that you will have some form of webinar or online discussion forum. This reflects the expectation that at master's level you will be part of a small learning group in which you are an active participant and in which everyone learns from each other. Remember Razvan's comment with which this book started:

'What I enjoyed most was the context of each seminar group as a unique laboratory of sharing and exchange – of ideas, views and theological perspectives.' The seminar group encourages individuals to take responsibility for their own learning and also to share this learning with others. It gives an opportunity through discussion to practise articulating and defending your own views to your peers. As a way of doing theology, the seminar group promotes 'empathy and imaginative insight, with a tolerance of diverse positions', which is one of the skills identified in the QAA Benchmark Statement for Theology and Religious Studies (QAA, 2007, p. 9).

## Being an effective seminar group member

What are the core skills of being a seminar group member?

- Be prepared. The tutor will very probably have asked you to read material in advance of the seminar. If you do not do this carefully, taking time over it, you will neither be able to contribute effectively nor perhaps even to understand what is going on. If several of the group don't prepare, the group cannot function.
- Be willing to listen to others attentively. Listening is a way to develop 'empathy and imaginative insight'. Through listening to others our own views are challenged and our horizons expanded.
- Observe 'netiquette' if you are involved in an online discussion group. Netiquette is etiquette for internet users. Your group may have its own rules, which you should observe. Beyond this there are some basic rules, which arise from the possible dangers of not being face to face with others, writing rather than speaking and working alone at your computer. Stay on the topic – don't ramble – and write clearly; never be abusive; don't

infringe copyright rules; remember what you say is at least in part public; make connections with what others are saying.

- Be willing to contribute – and to refrain from contributing. If you are nervous of contributing, try writing something down in advance that you might say. If you are someone who is always contributing, then try holding back a little so others get their turn. Remember that silence in the group may mean that the 'reflectors' are thinking out what they are going to say; if the 'activist' learners always jump in at their natural pace, then the 'reflectors' don't get a look in (Honey and Mumford, 1992). If you are using an online forum it is vital that you actually do make your contribution, regularly and by the date expected.

- Use 'and' not 'but'. Seminar groups can be intimidating and fruitless if they turn into one person trumping or demolishing the position of another. It is a good discipline to develop what someone else has said – 'and …', rather than show how wrong they are – 'but …'.

## Giving a seminar paper or other oral presentation

You may well be asked to give an oral presentation to the seminar group. This may be assessed. Websites, including university websites, offer many helpful tips on giving a presentation. One particularly clear and useful one is offered by London Metropolitan University (Londonmet). Here are some headline tips.

- Make sure you know what the expectations are for this particular presentation, especially the assessment criteria, if it is to be assessed. The tutor should give you this information.

- Keep to time. In order to do this you should practise before-hand. You may consider yourself an accomplished speaker already, but many such people go over time.
- Be well prepared – both in terms of content and in terms of how you will present your material in a digestible way.
- Do not try to cram too much in.
- If you use MSPowerPoint, use the slides imaginatively and do not overcrowd them. Pictures or diagrams can enhance your presentation.
- Speak slowly, clearly and audibly.

# Specific Learning Difficulties
# – Esther Shreeve

I am Esther Shreeve, and I worked in the Cambridge Theological Federation for 15 years, latterly as course director for an under-graduate programme and also as adviser and tutor for students with specific learning difficulties. So what is a SpLD? There are several, but the most common ones students may appear with are dyslexia, dyspraxia and attention deficit disorder (ADD). I did my teacher training in 1976, and at that stage none of these conditions was even on our radar, so it is not surprising that many of our mature students do not realize they may have a problem until they embark on their studies. Over the years such students may have subconsciously devised coping strategies to deal with their day-to-day difficulties. Faced with the demands of an academic course that involves cognitive processing, they may discover a need for extra support. Somewhere between five and ten per cent of the popula-tion are affected. Some may have been told at school that they were just not very bright – I had one student in her sixties who was told at primary school that she was educationally subnormal; she summoned up the courage to have a diagnostic assessment and found that she was quite severely dyslexic – but perfectly capable of studying at HE level, with specialist support.

The chances are that you do not have just one difficulty. It is not uncommon to find someone with a dyslexic profile but also with traits commensurate with ADD or dyspraxia (Turner and Rack, 2004, p. 86). There is no such thing as a 'typical dyslexic'. The way information is processed will be affected along with time management and personal organizational skills, the ability to read, understand, remember, marshal thoughts and plan assignments. All are essential study skills, and if a student is struggling with one or more of them, this will probably impact on their confidence, self-esteem and ability to cope with and enjoy the course.

Thankfully there is lots of help available. The most important thing is to recognize that there is a problem – talking this through with a tutor may help to pinpoint the problem areas, and the earlier this is done the better. The week before an assessment deadline is not the most opportune moment to confess to having a problem. Your university will have a Disability Centre. If you suspect or know that you have a SpLD, make an appointment as soon as possible to talk to one of the advisers. A diagnostic assessment with a specialist teacher or educational psychologist can be arranged for you, if this is appropriate.

If you are diagnosed with a SpLD, you will probably be entitled to support from the Disabled Students' Allowance (DSA), which will involve a further Needs Assessment and then the provision of appropriate IT equipment, software and quite possibly tutorial support from a specialist tutor. You may well need help to fill out the application form, however! Both full- and part-time students are eligible. One of my students commented after being assessed: 'I'm now looking forward to completing my studies to my full potential rather than having to work twice as hard as fellow students in order to get by.' Another observed: 'Esther equipped me with the organizational skills I needed, as well as helping me overcome the challenges of reading and essay writing.' The specialist tutor will not do your work for you, but will help you work on strategies that enable you to cope much better and that will help you for the rest of your life, long after you have finished your course.

Some students may choose not to go down the route of being assessed or applying for DSA, but there are several things you can do to help yourself.

- The most important thing is not to suffer in silence – talk to your tutors and explain you are having some difficulties. If time management is an issue for you, address it head on:
  - Make a planner for your week, either electronically or on paper.
  - Try using colour codes for different activities or places you have to be.
  - Make sure you put deadlines into your schedule, so you can work out your timing for assignments.
  - Most students find concentrating on one project at a time is easier than keeping several balls in the air at once.
  - Make sure you allow for time off and stick to it; working when you are tired is counterproductive.
- Ask for PowerPoint or other notes before the class, so you can be prepared. You can then re-format them into a font that works for you, allowing space for your own notes to be inserted as the class progresses. Printing the notes off on to a different colour paper may help, or altering the colour of your screen.
- If you are feeling overwhelmed by the amount of reading required, ask the lecturer to flag up the absolutely essential material and cut out the rest. Or make common cause with a

fellow student: divide up the reading, then compare notes over coffee and summarize what you have read for your friend. Ask your teachers to recommend podcasts, clips on YouTube and other auditory or visual resources relevant to your subject. As a church historian, I found Melvyn Bragg's *In Our Time* Radio 4 podcasts a great resource.

- When reading, making notes or planning for assignments, try to use a multisensory approach: the use of a digital recorder, coloured pens, highlighted text, sticky notes, mind-maps and so on can transform your learning. Hearing the text read aloud as well as reading it makes a difference, as in the Adobe 'read aloud' facility. Doodling while listening to something can be very helpful, particularly if you have ADD.

- The SuperReading course (originally aimed at businesses) has received some very good reviews from dyslexic students and tutors, and DSA may be used to fund it, if your assessor recommends.

- There is some good, free software available that can help with all of this, and there are links to this on the Diversity and Ability (DnA) site listed in the References and Further Resources section, along with some useful websites you might like to explore – of course, this is only accurate on the day I am writing, but the organization will probably still exist, even if the website has changed!

# 4

# Integrating Theory and Practice at Master's Level

This chapter is divided into three sections. The first discusses in terms appropriate to all theology master's degrees how personal stance, experience, tradition and theological theory may be related to one another. The second looks at models of action/reflection used in theology master's programmes, which are specifically designed in the field of practical or pastoral theology. The third addresses placement work.

## All theology is self-involving

All serious uses of theological language are ineluctably 'self-involving'. Or, as a friend of mine once put it, reading the scriptures is an exceedingly dangerous business. (Lash, 1988, p. 243)

## The dialectic of tradition and experience

When I was first doing postgraduate work in theology, a course was advertised called Integrating Tradition and Experience. I found the title compelling and attractive. It would, I assumed, enable me to make some sense out of my chaotic and changing relationship to the theology with which I had come to university and to the academic theology I was learning about. I was not prepared for what happened in the class, which was both one of the most disconcerting and one of the most profound learning experiences of my academic life. We sat in silence in a ring, until someone wished to speak. That was it, week in week out. It was not a therapy session, although it was jointly led by an academic theologian and a therapist/theologian. It was a radical move to allow the experiences of the people in the room to drive the agenda, as we wrestled with the relationship between our experience and the traditions of theology that had been handed down to us, by which we were surrounded and in which we were immersed. I cannot remember much of what happened except the long silences and the anger and fear expressed – people wanted to be 'taught' not to be thus thrown back on themselves.

The difficulty and the importance of that question have haunted me ever since. I would now put the issue not as *integrating* tradition and experience but as the *dialectic* of, or *tension* between, tradition and experience. Since those days I have spent much of my time teaching theology and running an MA in theology. I have noted that the struggle I had to relate traditions of theology to human experience, my own and that of others, is shared by those I now teach. This dialectic is central to learning in theology.

The views of nineteenth- and twentieth-century theologians Friedrich Schleiermacher (1768–1834) and Karl Barth (1886–1968) are often used to polarise the debate between those who start with human experience and those who start with God's revelation. Barth wrote of Schleiermacher, 'one cannot speak of God simply by speaking of man in a loud voice' (Barth, 1928, p. 196). They wrote in a particular European Protestant context, struggling with the legacy of the philosopher Immanuel Kant (1724–1804), who sought to demonstrate the sources of human knowing in the human being, and with the particularities of European culture and history, especially, in Barth's case, Germany in the two World Wars and the necessity to take a stand against tyranny. However, the debate about the sources of knowledge in theology they exemplify – that is, to prioritize the human or prioritize the revelation of God – finds its counterpart in other traditions.

Crudely put, we may take a position that prioritizes the authoritative voices of our theological tradition, for example the Bible, the Magisterium or the Liturgy; or we may take a stance that gives strong weight to these but also allows some questioning of them, or at least of our understanding of them, by the experiences we encounter in the world and in ourselves. Alongside this goes the questioning in reverse – the challenge to understand our experiences from the perspective of such authoritative voices. Or perhaps our standpoint might be that human experience is at the root of everything we can possibly know and that understandings of 'God', far from being transcendental revelation, arise from human experience. It is important to note that this debate is not primarily about whether we listen to God or to the human – it is about where we might most authentically *find* the voice of God. Barth did not accuse Schleiermacher of not wanting to speak of God but of looking for God in the wrong place. The dispute between the two Boff brothers, discussed in Chapter 6, exemplifies this well.

The so-called 'Wesleyan quadrilateral', naming Scripture, Tradition, Reason and Experience as the four sources of theology, expresses these points in a slightly different way. Reason is perhaps at first sight not parallel with the other elements as it is more a method than a source – Barth reputedly once said to a young man who asked him about the place of reason in his theology, 'I use it'. However, it is an important affirmation, from a Methodist point of view with its origins in Anglican thought and shared by some streams in most Christian traditions, that the exercise of human reason is one of God's good gifts to us and is not entirely blighted by the depravity of the human condition of fallenness.

It is crucial to recognize that as we come to our studies we come as people who are not clean slates but are already shaped by experiences and traditions. In our theological studies, we need to examine ourselves, what we bring with us to the table and to recognize how that will shape the whole course of our theological study. Experience, the interpretation of that experience, commitment to both the content and the methods of a theological or perhaps philosophical stance, are already embedded in us whether we recognize them or not. It is profoundly helpful to critical theological study to recognize and name all this. Try writing your own theological autobiography – how, why, when and where did I come to certain views? How have I changed? Who has influenced me? What are the key questions for me now and why are these key questions? Doing this will help you situate yourself within your own horizon and enable you to study in ways that engage with other horizons and can articulate how that engagement is taking place.

As a postgraduate student in the late 1980s I attended my first ever class that addressed issues in feminist theology. It was in a course on Theologians and Power. We were given as reading an article by Beverly Wildung Harrison on 'The Power of Anger in the Work of Love' (1990). Reading this article drew me into a maelstrom in which I had to address all the questions above. The first shock was emotional: Wildung Harrison was speaking about my personal experiences with an understanding I had never encountered before. Then the shock was theological: what she said challenged so many of my inherited theological beliefs and Christian practices and, vice versa, all these inherited beliefs and practices challenged some of what she was saying. The shock waves became wider than the personal – they became ecclesiological and political: this feminist theology engaged with what was going on around me in society and in the Church (the Church of England was in the throes of the ordination of women debate). This article and what followed it became part of something for me both painful, as I experienced a cognitive and emotional dissonance between tradition and experience, and creative, as I moved into new levels of understanding and new challenges to practice.

Both experiences, and traditions of interpretation of those experiences, form us, and they may both challenge us. The struggle or tension between tradition and experience may thus become a creative dialectic. We cannot escape either. There is no raw experience without some interpretation of that experience; both experience and interpretation – which may be handed down as tradition – go right through like lettering in a stick of rock. The study of theology requires us to work, sometimes painfully, with our old horizons and with our new ones.[1]

## Voices

In negotiating the dialectic of tradition and experience in an academic context, the 'four voices of theology' identified by Cameron et al. in their book, *Talking about God in Practice* (2010), are useful in disentangling issues and in finding a place from which to be critical. They name:

- normative theology – 'scriptures, creeds, official church teaching [and] liturgies'

---

1 For further discussion of relating tradition and experience, see Bennett, 2013, especially Chapter 3.

- formal theology – 'the theology of the theologians [and] dialogue with other disciplines'
- espoused theology – 'the theology embedded *within a group's articulation of its beliefs*'
- operant theology – 'the theology embedded *within the actual practices of a group*' (p. 54, Figure 4.2; emphasis in original).

For 'group' one can also of course also read 'individual', ourselves.

This typology allows several analytical and critical moves to be made in the context of the academic study of theology. It opens up a clear understanding of the difference between that body of material that is our inherited tradition and acts normatively for us, and the theoretical and often speculative writings of theologians. (In talking of 'normative' theology we should always remember that there is not one single Christian or any other religious tradition, and what is normative for us may not be for someone else.) Furthermore, it enables us to see that what people actually believe and practise may not be the same as either the official teachings or what the 'theologians' say. The recent spate of writing on 'ordinary theology' gives ample evidence of this (Astley and Francis, 2013). Finally, the typology invites us to consider that what people say, and even believe, that they practise and believe may not be what they actually do practise and believe. This will be as true of us and the groups/churches we belong to as it will of anyone else.

The possibility of hearing various voices, of distinguishing between them and of allowing them to ask critical questions of one another, opens up a disciplined way we can approach the chaos of the dialectic of tradition and experience and begin to lay out some of the key issues in any given topic or situation. It is an excellent analytical tool.

A rather different tool that also employs the idea of listening to voices is Jane Leach's idea of 'Theology as Attention' (Leach, 2007).

This model of doing theology commends disciplined attention to and reflection on a range of 'voices'. These include the actual voices heard in a situation, but also the voices of the Christian tradition, of a range of academic disciplines that can be brought into dialogue with theology, and not least of the self. As an analytical tool and heuristic device for critical engagement, its usefulness extends far beyond the specifically pastoral theological context in which it originated. Critical analysis is enabled by having a systematic and sustained framework through which that analysis is conducted. Such a framework offers us not only an ordered system for analysis but also suggests perspectives from which we can take a fresh view that challenges our current ideas – an important element in being critical.

## Reflexivity

Discussions on these themes will enable students to build a self-reflective view of theological identities, as well as engaging in debate on how Christian narratives could be and have been understood in contemporary society. This will include reflection on the students' own narratives and identity in the contexts of their communities.

These words are taken from the description of the Cambridge Theological Federation's core module for its MA in Christian Theology, which is focused on doctrine, Bible and missiology. Reflexivity is an important component of all theological work, not just of pastoral or practical theology. The meanings given to the terms 'reflective' and 'reflexive' in published work are not always consistent. Being 'reflective' normally means looking thoughtfully at something – usually at some length, with the benefit of hindsight and with a critical eye. Being 'self-reflective' or 'reflexive' normally means specifically looking thoughtfully at one's own self – at what I am like, at how I see what is outside of myself, how I affect it or how my seeing of it affects how I present it.

It is a common mistake to confuse 'subjectivity' with lack of a critical perspective or academic credibility. When I ask how we might be more critical, students often reply that we need to be more 'objective'. This is a half-truth at best. It is well attested across a range of contemporary academic disciplines that you cannot split the knower and the known object cleanly or completely. This has spawned all kinds of fascinating theological debates but these are not our concern here. What is our concern is that our subjective viewpoint and the context in which it arises not only cannot be dispensed with, but it can be an aid to knowledge not a barrier. This positive gain, however, is entirely dependent on our willing-ness and our ability to examine our viewpoint and context and to explore how they are yielding a particular perspective on the object under scrutiny. If 'the truth looks different from here', it becomes crucial to examine 'here' (Soskice, 1993). What we are looking for is not a detached objectivity but a *critical* subjectivity.

However, reflexivity, or looking at oneself, is a complex task. Let us examine it through two contrasting images. The first is Caravaggio's painting of Narcissus: the luminous boy looking with yearning at the reflection that only just comes into focus; the danger of what he is doing and the compelling delight of it. Such 'narcissism' has its dangers, not least the difficulties of seeing that which is ugly, inconsistent, inadequate or painful to know. It requires a certain distance to overcome the fuzziness, though the boy tries to get a clearer picture simply by coming ever nearer. Narcissus is poised on the brink of falling into the water, becom-ing one with his own reflection, fatally losing forever any critical space between himself and what he sees. So the first danger is of so much closeness that we fail to see ourselves with critical distance.

The second danger is that we tell too simple a story – as if there is merely a single reflection and no complexity about ourselves in relation to our context. Consider a second image: Anish Kapoor's 'Bean' in Chicago.[2] This is a huge public sculpture with a highly reflective surface of seamless stainless steel plates, curved and shaped like a bean (its real title is *Cloud Gate*). It reflects and distorts – in changing patterns dependent on where you are standing – the Chicago skyline, the masses of people around it and the individual viewer, who is likely to be taking a photograph of themselves taking a photograph of themselves reflected in the sculpture. It is a wonderful image of the complexity and the multifaceted, potentially distorted and changing nature of reflexivity. In seeking to reflect on ourselves and our context and on how this affects how we see that to which we attend in theology, these two images may serve as exploratory devices to think through the nature of the task and its complexity.

# Pastoral/Practical/Contextual/Applied Theology

## Reflective practice

Many master's degrees in theology are set up so that those engaged in practical ministry or pastoral care may reflect on their practice, in engagement with fellow practitioners, with staff and with written texts and theoretical perspectives. This 'reflective practice'

---

2 Both images are easily accessible through Google Images.

element may of course be found at undergraduate level, but it is a particular characteristic of many master's programmes, not only in theology but in other vocationally orientated subject areas such as music therapy or social work. What does it mean to study for a degree in which practical experience is part of the material for learning and needs to be integrated with theoretical material? Some such master's degrees have a high level of placement time allocated within the degree itself; others expect you to bring the experience with you or to have it ongoing in other parts of your life while you are studying part-time.

For some people this practical element is just what they need, allowing them to bring their skills and practical experience into an academic context perhaps for the first time and to flourish. Others find it harder. On the one hand, some struggle to see how practice can be connected to theory and long for a good old-fashioned essay that can be argued out of a few books. On the other hand, some practitioners find making the move into theoretical thinking difficult and demanding. At master's level a serious critical engagement with theoretical texts is expected in relation to practice in respect of all assessment tasks. There may be some exceptions but check carefully; it is most unusual if this is not expected. Alongside this a seriously reflective approach to your own practice is required. And as if two tasks were not enough, a sustained connection between the two must be made. In these three tasks there are some models which may help you.

The basic model of what has come to be known as the 'pastoral cycle' is a movement from practice/experience to analysis and on again, in fact more like a spiral than a circle (see Figure 3). This model and its use in practical theology has several rather different though intertwined roots, and it is helpful to understand these and identify which of them is strongest both in the course you are enrolled in and in your own thinking and practice.

## Figure 3 The pastoral cycle

renewed practice

experience

engagement with the theological tradition

description of that experience

analysis of that experience

One root is in the educational tradition of experiential learning (Kolb, 1984). This tradition emphasizes that the way human beings learn is through their own experience and through reflection on that experience. Other learning remains at a shallow or superficial level. A second root is in the professional tradition of the development of the reflective, therefore effective, practitioner (Schön, 2003). Miller-McLemore (1999, p. 87) has suggested that practitioners, including pastoral practitioners, may have a tendency to conservatism – this is the way I do it and it works – and may thus be less effective than they could be. A third root is in movement to return research and the development of theory and practice to the practitioners. This is has a strong tradition in the public service professions (see a most useful and practical book by Helen Kara, 2012). Finally, a root with which many of you will be familiar is liberation theology, which uses the Marxian concept of praxis to encourage reflection on practices in order to interrogate those practices, to inform action and to facilitate change and transformation of society (Boff, 1987; Freire, 1972).

It is important to understand these different roots to see that there may be many different motivations in using the pastoral cycle. These may be to do with effectiveness of practice or with transformation of society. The two are not the same. They may be to do with a pedagogical understanding of *how* we learn or a theological commitment to God's revelation coming to us through human experience – again very different. Using the pastoral cycle doesn't automatically make you a Marxist, nor does it prevent you holding a high view of God's revelation through the Bible or the Church. Such political, philosophical or theological commitments are logically independent from using the pastoral cycle as a method of reflection.

What a commitment to reflective practice does imply is that theology is contextual. It is to parody the situation to contrast a classical or catholic (in the sense of universal) theology, entirely 'top down', totally independent of context, timeless and unchanging, with a contextual theology that is 'from below', shaped by context, develops and changes (see Vassiliadis, no date). The reality is that the beliefs and practices that make up our faith are constantly lived out in context and inculturated. There are, however, some sharp differences in how we might envisage the relationship between theory/theology and practice, ranging from a commitment to accepting what is 'authorized' in Scripture or Tradition and applying it in context, through an explicit wrestling to allow the tradition to interpret context and the context to interpret tradition, to a full 'turn to practice' in which practice is seen as the prime locus of theological disclosure.

## Action/reflection models

The basic shape of an experiential learning cycle is to start with experience, move through analysis and reflection and come to renewed and changed practice. The specific version of this that has been developed in practical theology (see Figure 3) owes much to its roots in liberation theology. The rationale for this is set out in Clodovis Boff's magisterial *Theology and Praxis* (1987).[3] Boff contends that it is the work of theology to be engaged with the realities of this world, that is with practice. But, he says, it is inappropriate to try to bring theology to bear on the supposed realities of this world without first examining and analysing those supposed realities to see them more clearly and truly. So, for example, in his own South American context an understanding and analysis of poverty in national and global contexts offers the material on which to reflect theologically. Trying to skip the analysis stage risks reflecting on a distorted picture of reality. This yields the process of first describing what is encountered, then analysing it with the tools of the human sciences such as sociology and psychology, then reflecting theologically on what has been unearthed and then moving on to renewed practice in a renewed understanding. It is crucial to see that the placing of analysis by the human sciences before theological reflection is not to prioritize the human sciences over theology but to acknowledge that what we first see may have hidden dimensions that we need to unearth in order to examine them theologically.

In working with the material that you bring to your master's assignments it is helpful to use some sort of structure for reflection. Many suggested structures are available in the literature of

---

3 Of which I give an account in *The Cambridge Companion to Liberation Theology* (Bennett, 2007). See Laurie Green (2009) for a readable and influential pioneering account in a UK context.

practical theology, of which I mention only a selection. Some are designed more for group reflection, especially when that group is actively involved in a practical project of some sort (North-cott, 2000; Lartey, 2000); others are more easily used individually (Farley, 2000 and Lyall, 2000 as a worked example of this; Leach, 2007; Pattison, 2000). Some offer particular ways of engaging with theology – for example, Farley suggests looking at the situation through the lenses of corruption and redemption, as these are key to the Christian understanding of reality. Leach places strong emphasis on the ecclesial dimension of practice and on prayer. What following such a structure does is to discipline your attention into considering matters you might easily skip over. Furthermore, it enables you to write a well-structured essay in a field where it is easy to wander all over the place. It is important to choose your method carefully to be appropriate to your material and your context and interests. It is also vital to state why you have chosen this method and indeed to critique how well it worked for you. Justifying your choices of method and evaluating them in this way raises the level of your work significantly and is expected in master's degrees.

Behind the specific models offered lie a range of approaches to doing practical theology and theological reflection within it. At master's level it is good to take your thinking up to this level – not only what model am I using but what kind of approach am I taking that lies behind my choice and use of a model?[4] Ballard and Pritchard, in their useful introductory *Practical Theology in Action* (2006, chapter 5), describe a range of approaches to doing practical theology – applied theory, critical correlation, praxis and habitus. Bevans (2002) offers five models of the relationship between the-ology and cultural context that may lie behind our theological

---

4 These questions approximate to the 'methods' and 'methodology' of empirical research.

engagement – the translation model, the anthropological, praxis, the synthetic model and the transcendental. Graham, Walton and Ward (2005) suggest seven methods of doing theological reflection – 'theology by heart', constructive narrative theology, canonical narrative theology, corporate theological reflection ('writing the body of Christ'), correlation, praxis and 'theology in the vernacular'; that is, local theology. Identifying the approach you are using within one of these typologies encourages you to stand back and look at what you are doing and why you are doing it this way, and to analyse and critique it. This is an important skill in academic work. Indeed, looking at such analyses of how theology is engaged with the world may creatively suggest ideas to you of how you might pursue your assignments.

## The personal and the anecdotal

These models require you to talk about yourself. They explicitly invite you to position yourself within the situation examined and/ or to examine the attitudes, the emotions, the intellectual stance and the theological commitments that you bring to a situation and to theological reflection on it. This encourages the kind of reflexivity and critical subjectivity required in practical theology.

But this raises some questions. Can I use 'I'? How do I avoid being anecdotal? These are two questions I am frequently asked. I discussed the use of the first-person pronoun more generally above (see p. 24), but in the context of practical theological reflection it is not only permissible, it is normally essential. You are likely to be writing about your own practice; you may well be invited to keep a journal; you will often be asked to reflect on your own involvement. Naming and speaking of yourself is essential.

More complex is the question of the 'anecdotal'. The *Collins*

*English Dictionary* defines 'anecdotal' as 'containing or consisting exclusively of anecdotes rather than connected discourse or research conducted under controlled conditions'. Several features of this definition indicate both what is wrong with being anecdotal and also how to avoid it.

The definition points to the absence of 'connected discourse'. In an academic piece of work you should always aim for connected discourse – that is to say, you should aim to build up your arguments in a way that explores them thoroughly and moves through connected steps to conclusions. Your work should show coherence – that the various elements hang together, how they hang together and why they hang together. Other common mistakes that make writing insufficiently connected, in addition to the disconnected accumulation of anecdotes, are over-use of bullet points and the use of too-short paragraphs (fewer than three sentences is normally too short).

Lack of research conducted under controlled conditions is the other element of this definition of 'anecdotal'. If you wish to give evidence of something in your work that carries weight beyond the single individual example itself, then you need to do one of two things. You either need to quote and reference research others have undertaken and published or you need to do research yourself in a way that reflects the methodological and ethical standards expected in rigorous research, and normally you will not be able to do this unless you have received some training in research methods (see Chapter 8). Please note that this doesn't mean you cannot do small-scale locally contextual research; it just means you need to do research according to accepted standards of rigour.

This is to put the negative side of the term 'anecdotal', but there is a positive side too. The same dictionary goes on to define an 'anecdote' as 'a short, usually amusing account of an incident, especially a personal or biographical one'. To use such accounts in academic work is not necessarily inappropriate. At my PhD viva the first question I was asked by my examiners was one that appreciated my use of amusing stories and asked me about their role in practical theology. It all depends on your purpose in using such stories. Anecdotal material may raise issues in a way that shows their relevance to real life. Such stories may move the reader to laugh or cry, to understand the affective/emotional side of an issue, or they may help you and your reader to appreciate a different angle on something. Perhaps the account of the incident might be a way for you to move into further exploration of the issues it raises. All of these are legitimate uses of short personal accounts or anecdotes.

I therefore consider that the automatic wholesale rejection of the anecdotal is not appropriate. Especially in pastoral or practical theology, where there is a commitment to look seriously at experience, there is a place for concentrating on the specific individual incidence. Generalization is not always required, for generalization may move us away from the 'minute particulars' of life that it is the business of the practical theologian to see well and to explore. Nevertheless, the warnings against unconnected argument or unfounded research claims should be seriously heeded.

## Placement work

It is often in placement work of different kinds that students find the integration of theory and practice most difficult. At first sight this may seem strange, but I think that there are some good reasons for this phenomenon. I hope that looking at them might at least forewarn and forearm you.

A placement may be connected with a judgement being made about your fitness to practise, for example as an ordained person or as a chaplain. This focuses the mind on the practical things that must be done well, which may be either rather frightening or possibly a great relief after the more theoretical elements of your course. It is, of course, extremely important to concentrate on those elements of good practice in the assessment criteria for the module, but this should not be at the expense of the requirements to reflect and to engage with relevant literature.

In founding the Clinical Pastoral Education movement, Anton Boisen (1876–1965) was concerned that those training for ministry might have the opportunity to engage not only with the 'living human document' out there (other people) but with the living human document inside (ourselves and our own emotions). He had himself spent time in hospital dealing with issues of personal mental health and knew these were places ministers needed to learn about and come to terms with (Shipani, 2011). New experiences in placements can be disorientating, even frightening, and can demand a great deal of you and exhaust you. The verbatims or journals that you might be required to produce are not easy work. You may feel you have little heart or head space for reading secondary literature or engaging critically, but this is also necessary and in fact may help you in gaining a critical space from which to view your experiences.

Sometimes the guidelines for what is expected of placement work are not sufficiently clear; or perhaps they are clear to the writer of them but not clear to you the reader. I experienced an example of excellent practice in clarity of guidelines when I was doing my teaching training. We were asked:

- to choose a theoretical description of how communication works from one of our textbooks;
- to choose an example of miscommunication from our own teaching;

- to analyse what happened in our classroom according to the theoretical framework chosen.

This was a rich and complex task to do but it was very clear what was expected. If you are in doubt about how you are expected to integrate theory and practice in your context, do ask for guidance.

In sum, when you are doing placement work, try using the following checklist:

- Get absolute clarity about what is expected of you and of any practical, oral or written work you are doing for assessment.
- Check your bibliography – have you included a range of secondary reading that has enabled you to reflect on your practical work?
- Use specific action/reflection models – some may be advised in specific modules. So often I have seen the comment on a student's placement work: 'Excellent quality of personal reflection, but little engagement with the literature.' Sometimes I have seen the opposite: 'This is an excellent essay, but it could have been written from your desk and reflects nothing of the placement itself.' Good quality of personal reflection on the actual realities of the placement, together with engagement with other traditions, viewpoints and theories, make for first-class placement work. Using a model for reflection on practice will help.
- Ask yourself how you have been able to look critically at your own personal practice and prior assumptions/beliefs – through what lenses? Make clear to the assessor how you have approached this.

# Conclusion

I have a poster on my office door that reads: 'Theory is when you understand everything and nothing works. Practice is when everything works but you don't understand why. Here we have brought the two together: nothing works and no one knows why!' I hope that this chapter has helped to put you in the opposite position. All theology is about both experiences and practices and about understanding reasons behind things, the 'Why?', 'faith seeking understanding'. Practical, pastoral, applied or contextual theology, in different ways, require explicit engagement with the relationship between theory and practice. The placement is an academic context in which this engagement may be actually enacted as part of work on a master's degree.

# 5

# Being Scholarly

The QAA document I quoted in Chapter 1 refers to the master's graduate as someone who has:

> an in-depth knowledge and understanding of the discipline informed by current scholarship and research, including a critical awareness of current issues and developments in the subject.

Further, a master's graduate will be able to:

> communicate effectively, with colleagues and a wider audience, in a variety of media. (QAA, 2010, pp. 13–14)

Doing a master's degree is a bridge into a scholarly and researching community, whether or not you intend to become an academic researcher or a reflective and enquiring practitioner. This means that you need to show how your work relates to current debates in the area you are looking at; that you need to write in a style appropriate to the academic study of your discipline; and that the form in which your work is presented needs to adhere to scholarly conventions.

The consistent use of 'scholarly conventions' is a common assessment criterion for master's work. You may well find it listed in the assessment criteria your university states. What is meant by 'scholarly conventions'? The following are some key elements.

- Spelling and grammar have been corrected.
- An abstract has been supplied, if expected, in the format required.
- If the work you are presenting has an established format – for example, the 'literature review, methodology, findings, discussion' format of a typical piece of research in social sciences – you present your work in that way. The description of your assignment in the module guide may have such a format laid out; it is important to keep to it and fulfil all the expectations.
- All the work of others to which you refer or from which you quote is properly referenced.
- The tone of voice or register in which you write is appropriate to an academic piece of work.

This chapter addresses three essential aspects of what it means to work in a scholarly way that communicates to those who will read your work and meets standard requirements at master's level. The first concerns the use in academic work of primary and secondary sources. The second concerns how those sources need to be quoted and referenced. The third concerns writing style. I will use three passages taken from published work to demonstrate the issues.

Friedrich Schleiermacher (1768–1864) is responsible for what many regard as the definitive categorization of theological studies in the academy and is the theologian from whom several significant trends in modern pastoral and practical theology can be traced. Schleiermacher set about providing a coherent rationale with the publication in 1811 of his theological encyclopaedia *A Brief Outline on the Study of Theology* (Schleiermacher, 1966). This was essentially an attempt to re-establish the scientific status of theology and its epistemological claims by locating the study of theology in the service of the Christian Church. The community of faith was primary for Schleiermacher, serving as the critical point of reference for the truth-claims and relevance of the scholarly study of theology.

(Graham, 1996, p. 59)

On holiday in Brittany I sat one morning by a grave over 5,000 years old. At the mouth of the Jaudy Estuary the 'covered alley' of Men ar Rompet lies on the headland, huge lichen encrusted stones roofing the narrow chamber. How did they lift such stones? I wanted to photograph them but somehow that didn't capture enough. As I lingered I began to wonder – why did I want to record, to describe? Three of Ruskin's four reasons applied: so I could go on remembering them; to convey them to others; that by looking more attentively I might enter more deeply into their reality.[1] As I sat and looked I felt drawn to think of the lives and deaths of those who were buried there so long ago. They looked out on the beautiful headland, sea and estuary, as from their graves my mother and father look out over the hills of Galloway, and my son over the trees and park in Bedford and my brother over the wide Essex cornfields. I realized that in addition to lingering and looking with precision, to walking round and considering ,to describing accurately ,there is human sympathy –a sense of the  tears of things', Virgil's 'lacrimae rerum', community of spirit with all things human. Ruskin had this supremely. To know him or any human being more intimately, he said, we must learn to read the 'torn manuscripts of the human soul'.[2] Although it is a prerequisite, seeing clearly is not enough; we need 'heart-sight' as well as eyesight.[3]

[1] Chapter 6, p. 84.
[2] *Works* 18, p. 28.
[3] *Works* 7, p. 377.

(Bennett, 2013, p. 89)

Human beings, says Clifford Geertz in a famous image, are animals suspended in webs of significance they themselves have spun.[1] 'Culture' is the name for those webs. It is what we make of the world, materially, intellectually and spiritually. These dimensions cannot be separated: the Word is necessarily flesh. In constructing the world materially we interpret it, set values on it. To talk of values is to talk of a culture's self-understanding, its account of its priorities. The everyday world, the built environment, rituals, symbols, ideals and practices all rest on these values. At the end of his discussion of cultural imperialism John Tomlinson remarks that the failure of modernity is a specifically cultural one, namely the inability to decide what people should value, believe in and what sense they ought to make of their everyday lives.[2] 'Values set down final standards for desired social relations, individual modes of behaviour, social and political structures, life goals and ideals for the individual and the collective self. Furthermore, they also bind people's feelings and guide their moral judgement.'[3] Culture, we can say, is concerned with the spiritual, ethical and intellectual significance of the material world. It is, therefore, of fundamental theological concern.

1 C. Greetz, *The Interpretation of Cultures*, London: Fontana, 1993, p. 5
2 J. Tomlinson, *Cultural Imperialism*, London: Continuum, 1991, p. 169
3 T. Meyer, *Identity Mania: Fundamentalism and the Politicisation of Cultural Differences*, London: Zed, 2001, p. 71

(Gorringe, 2004, p. 3)

The first of these extracts is from an early chapter of Elaine Graham's *Transforming Practice* (1996) that lays out historical perspectives on pastoral theology. The second is from my own book, *Using the Bible in Practical Theology* (2013), and is from the central part of the book that invites the reader to engage with the work of John Ruskin as a way of understanding issues in relating the Bible to our own context. The third extract is the opening paragraph of Timothy Gorringe's *Furthering Humanity: A Theology of Culture* (2004). Before reading what I have to say about these passages, try asking yourself a few questions.

- Which of these pieces do you most warm to and why?
- How would you characterize each piece?
- Can you identify specific details of the style of each?
- Look at how the referencing is done – what are the differences?
- How does each author use other literature?

# 'Informed by current scholarship and research': the use of primary and secondary sources

We will look in turn at how each of our authors use primary and secondary material to inform their theoretical frameworks and to give sources of their information and evidence for what they say.

Graham is dealing with a primary source. Note how she gives dates for an author who is not contemporary. This is especially important as the date of publication of the recent version of his work, 1966, might give the impression he was a twentieth-century author. She contextualizes Schleiermacher, letting the reader know something about his work and his concerns. Graham's detailed information and her reference to a primary source give us confidence that she is in control of the material she is using and has chosen it carefully to make her point about the importance of Schleiermacher for pastoral theology. I think in a master's level essay it would be wise also to give a secondary source – maybe Graham herself! – as evidence for such a reading of Schleiermacher, and indeed to note whether this is a standard reading or if some current scholars would dispute it. The key issue is that we establish that we have good grounds for asserting what we say.

In my piece I also use a primary source, John Ruskin. I refer to his work three times. The first time I refer back to a previous chapter and take further the material I had considered then, concerning the reasons for drawing. It is good to build up an argument using our sources – not just to make a single point then drop them. The second two references involve actual quotations. The first of these quotations reinforces the point I am making about emotional engagement. The second, though it is actually only literally the quotation of a single word, 'heart-sight' as set against mere eyesight, is in the final sentence of the paragraph and constitutes its conceptual punchline. Everything I have said in this paragraph is to lead the reader into an understanding of what I mean by 'seeing with the heart' (the title of the chapter). Note how the argument is mine; Ruskin is used to develop that argument. I indicate a deep knowledge of my sources here and a capacity to deploy them in the service of *my* argument.

Two further points can be made about this extract. The first concerns the use of the quotation from Virgil. Here I have used a well-known phrase from a classic writer to add imaginative and conceptual punch to what I am writing. I have made the judgement that it is enough of a 'classic' not to need referencing and also that it is better for the reader if I use an English translation as well as the Latin. Both these judgement calls might have been made differently by someone else. You need to be very careful about the use of a foreign language in a piece of work submitted in English, particularly if you are using a text not published in English. You need to translate any quotations and references, though you may give them in the original as well.

The second point is that in this extract there is no reference to contemporary scholarship about Ruskin, nothing that shows whether my interpretation of him is standard, original or even disputed. The reader/marker can rightly expect this in other parts of the book/essay. The use of primary sources that are not contemporary needs to be complemented by the use of up-to-date scholarship both on the general subject and on how that scholarship treats our primary sources.

Gorringe's opening remarks locate him thoroughly and directly in contemporary scholarship. He chooses to start with a striking image, not directly quoted but referenced, from an acknowledged key scholar in the field. In this opening paragraph he refers to three scholars (though note that in only one case does he directly quote), while retaining the thrust and drive of his own argument throughout. The final sentence of the paragraph is his own programmatic statement, in his own words, for the importance of the subject matter of the book that is to come.

There is extensive use of secondary literature here; however, this does not overwhelm Gorringe's own argument. Why is this? I suggest three reasons. The first is that his main point, concerning the fundamental theological concern of culture, is his own. Second, he *uses* the secondary literature to explain what he means and indeed thus to exclude what he does not mean, by the key concept for his work, 'culture'. This use of secondary literature to establish what we mean by a word or a concept can often be helpful. Third (and this is a point about style also), he begins 'Human beings …'; he does not begin 'Clifford Geertz says'. The difference is enormous. Gorringe is writing about human beings; he is not writing about Clifford Geertz. So his first words are 'human beings', and 'human beings' are the *subject* of the sentence. Beware of making a secondary author the subject of your sentence unless you really are writing about that author as the main subject of your argument at that point.

Using primary and secondary sources is very important in academic writing. It establishes our work in research and scholarship, including contemporary research and scholarship. It is generally thought that going to secondary sources first is wiser as this enables you to understand the primary sources better and to contextualize them. However, a disadvantage of this is that you come to the primary sources with less of an open mind and less able to see fresh and exciting things in them. You may need therefore to move back and forth between primary and secondary sources to optimize a good critical perspective.

The research and scholarship of others is not a substitute for your own. None of the extracts we have considered uses many long verbatim quotations. These should be avoided as they are often a lazy way of using someone else to make what should be your argument. A rule of thumb is that if you use a long quotation, your discussion of it should be twice as long as the quotation. Furthermore, you should choose the 'research and scholarship' you use carefully – do you know this is a reliable source (especially important for the use of material found on the internet), is it a significant source, a respected source? What is the context of your source – date, perspective of author, geographical and cultural context? Without knowing these things and demonstrating that you know them, it is not possible to use your sources in a way that is apt for your argument and persuasive to the reader.

# Referencing sources correctly

Why is it necessary to reference our sources correctly? There are several reasons. The first is that when we use other people's ideas or words it is unethical to do so without acknowledging that these ideas or words are not our own. We should not pass them off as our own and take the credit for them, which would be deception and cheating. Second, we often use the ideas or words or indeed information of others to lend authority to and evidence for what we are saying. If we do not indicate clearly the sources of such material, it lends no authority at all – we could have made it up. This takes us to the reasons for full and clear referencing: readers must be able to trace the sources we are using, go to these sources themselves and check out what we are saying or follow up ideas.

All of this indicates that we need a system for referencing that is full and clear and consistently used. The reader needs to be able to make a direct move from our in-text reference or footnote to the relevant place in our reference list at the end, and to identify with ease what is the source we are using. All systems of referencing recommended by universities and by publishers are designed to achieve this. Fortunately we do not need to work this out on our own. Universities normally prescribe one particular way and give excellent guidance in how it works. This will be found on your university's website, often in the library section. It is expected that you will follow exactly the system of referencing sources and quotations required by your university.

Referencing is an unnecessary stumbling block to many students. Adhering absolutely to your university's prescribed method in every jot and tittle is foundational to receiving a good mark. It is a shame that when it is such a routine task, for which we are spoon-fed by the website information, so many people don't bother to do it. Their work is the poorer for this and marks are dropped. Quite apart from the intrinsic importance of referencing properly, there is an interesting correlation between care over referencing and care over other aspects of work – and markers know this. By referencing properly you send out a signal that you have taken care over your work.

There are many different ways of referencing, as you will know from the articles and books you read and as you can see in the extracts I have given. The two main systems are author-date (as in the Graham extract and as in this book) and footnotes (as in the Bennett and Gorringe extracts). Even within each of these there are differences, greater or smaller – see, for example, how Gorringe's footnotes do not have a full stop at the end whereas mine do! Note also that the referencing of a primary work – as Ruskin *Works* in my case – may have special requirements. You do not need to worry about this – each instance will be exemplified in the guidelines; all you need to worry about is doing exactly what your own university requires.

I mentioned above that passing off someone else's work as your own is a form of cheating. It is known as 'plagiarism'. Most universities regard this as an assessment offence, and it is variously penalized and, if persistent, regarded as a disciplinary offence. They normally state clearly in their regulations, and often in module guides, exactly what plagiarism is and what the penalties for it are. Sometimes there are some blurred edges between poor academic practice and plagiarism, but if you do the following you will not be plagiarizing: always put quotation marks around all words quoted from someone else and make a reference to the exact page number (or other place indicator) in the document from which the words are taken. Common mistakes that can lead to plagiarism are:

- to think that someone else's words are better than yours and more authoritative, and so to use them without saying they are someone else's;
- to forget to put material in quotation marks when you copy it from a book or cut and paste it from the internet – then later you think it was your notes;
- to forget to note the reference for such material, especially the page number, and not to have the time or energy later to go back and check;
- to be in such a hurry you panic and just stick in other people's material (such as Wikipedia), hoping no one will spot it;
- to put quotation marks round a small part of the quotation but not the whole of it;
- to use tables or bullet-point lists from other sources and forget that these also need quotation marks and referencing;
- to think you are paraphrasing – writing someone else's argument in your own words – when actually you are just changing the odd word here and there.

There are some good instruments for checking plagiarism available both to you and to your markers, for example Turnitin, which is a piece of online educational technology designed for this purpose. It is worth seeing whether your university offers a service whereby you can check your work before you submit it.

Notice that in the extracts above, secondary sources are used in differing ways. Graham refers to Schleiermacher's work in a general way that only requires a reference to the whole book. Gorringe uses summaries of very particular sections of Geertz's and Tomlinson's work that certainly require page numbers to indicate where the material is from. '[S]uspended in webs of significance' is actually a direct quotation, and I would have advised a master's student to use quotation marks, although of course Gorringe's text makes it absolutely clear that he has taken the image from Geertz's work, and on which page it is to be found, so he is in no way passing the image off as his own. Indeed on the contrary, he is deliberately locating his work in a classic tradition of the understanding of culture (as Geertz has taken the image from Max Weber). Bennett and Gorringe use direct quotations that clearly require page numbers. It is also interesting in passing to note that in Gorringe's first reference footnote there is a spelling error. Avoid errors in references if you possibly can – they need to be checked as much as the main text. Markers may spot-check page numbers of references. Put more positively: correctly and consistently referenced work indicates a scholarly attitude and practice on your part, which will be rewarded.

# Style and voice

The style or tone of voice in which any given piece of academic work is written depends on several factors. The first is the person doing the writing. Another is the requirements of this particular piece of writing – this section, chapter or perhaps whole work. I have already written extensively about the art of writing in Chapter 2. Here I propose to concentrate on the particular issues that arise in relation to the three extracts we are examining.

It is interesting to do some empirical research on these three extracts. Consider the following questions:

- How many words are in each sentence?
- What parts of speech do the sentences start with?
- How many adjectives, adverbs, nouns and verbs are used?
- Does the author use the kinds of word for which you might need a dictionary? What are these?

- How are the author's sentences built up?

All these features contribute to the style, tone and voice of the work. For example, Graham's sentences are all between 26 and 37 words long; Bennett's sentences (note how I change the tone by referring to myself as Bennett whereas earlier I used 'I'; neither is wrong) are 4–43 words long; Gorringe's sentences are 7–44 words long, but note that of 12 sentences only four are more than 17 words long. The different word lengths change the voice. Graham's voice is measured, authoritative and explanatory. She is using this passage to convey (historical) information and to lay the ground for her later argument to develop. My voice is rhetorical, with an eye on persuading my readers and drawing them in to understand the key idea of my chapter. Gorringe's voice is punchy. He wants his readers to be very clear from the start what he is talking about, why he is justified in talking about it and why it is important – to catch their interest and belief that he can deliver something worthwhile right from the beginning of his book. The sentence lengths play a significant part in achieving these various effects.

The pieces I have chosen do use words and sentences that require serious thought and attention. Graham uses 'epistemologically' which, as I pointed out in Chapter 2, is a word theologians need to know; Gorringe uses a range of concepts, such as 'symbols' and 'imperialism', which are important for cultural studies and theology. I use a quotation from a Latin classic, which might require some readers to follow it up to contextualize it. None of the passages, however, contains convoluted sentences or long and obscure words.

Nor are any of the pieces chatty. Mine is personal, yes, but not colloquial or chatty. If anything, I had to construct it more carefully and with more artifice, precisely because it was so personal, and I was trying to introduce a complex concept via a personal story.

It is important to edit your work to make sure it has a thoughtful and careful tone and says well what you want it to say. This is just as true of a reflective piece, such as a learning journal, as it is of an essay where much of your material is secondary, or a piece of empirical research where you have a prescribed methodology and results to convey and discuss.

Being scholarly covers a multitude of virtues, from developing your thinking in the context of current research and scholarship to presenting that work in a way that communicates this and accords with expected conventions of referencing and style. Being scholarly is not about being a conformist who cannot think for themselves; on the contrary, it is about learning some tools of the trade that enable you to speak out confidently in a voice that communicates what you have to offer in the best possible way.

# 6

# Commitment versus Critique

## Introduction

Many, though not all, theological students come to their studies with prior faith commitments (Cargas et al., 2005). If you are in this situation, this chapter is for you; others may like to skip it or may read on for interest. A key expectation of academic work in higher education in the UK is that the candidate will be 'critical'. If you look at the expected learning outcomes for master's courses and for specific modules within them, you will repeatedly see the terms 'critical analysis' or 'evaluation'. Analysis implies breaking something down and looking at it; evaluation implies making judgements about something; the word 'critical' suggests perhaps a willingness to be negative in that evaluation, suspicious in that analysis. Such attitudes towards our dearly treasured beliefs, and towards those texts and institutions that mediate our beliefs to us, may feel difficult, perhaps sacrilegious, threatening and indeed inappropriate. How do we square faithfulness to our religious commitments with the demands of higher education?

This issue may be made even more complicated if you are work-ing in an ecumenical or interfaith context, where the different perspectives and the questions of people who hold to your faith in a different way or to other faiths offer challenges that are uncom-fortable (Bennett, 2004). You may be asked to consider questions, the very asking of which feels disloyal to your own tradition. This may be made yet more painful if you have also crossed cultural divisions, and Chapter 7 is especially devoted to exploring issues for international students.

There are two issues embedded in these questions, which I will explore in this chapter. The first is about how we inhabit our tradition trustfully while also feeling free enough to ask the kinds of questions the context of our master's study requires of us. The second, related, question is about how we negotiate between the submission to authority some religious traditions expect of us – for example to the Bible or to the teachings of the Church – and our own independent critical thinking and questioning, on the basis of experience or reason or of different viewpoints brought by others. There are no simple answers to these questions, so starting with stories of how others in various different traditions have faced them might get us thinking. It might be helpful to think of the attitudes that may lie behind critique and commitment. What are we prepared to be suspicious of? What are we prepared to trust?

# Suspicion and trust

## A quarrel over liberation theology

Sandro Magister tells the story of public quarrel between the Boff brothers, Clodovis and Leonardo (Magister, 2008). Both brothers had been instrumental in the development of liberation theology in Latin America, but now they were taking different views on the sources of authority for theology. Clodovis had published a work that indicated that '[i]n his judgment, the "fatal" error into which it [liberation theology] falls is that of setting up the poor as the "first operative principle of theology," substituting them for God and Jesus Christ'. Writing of a document of the 'Latin American bishops at their continental conference held in Aparecida, Brazil, in May of 2007 and inaugurated by Benedict XVI in person', he says:

> This document ... is a 'clear demonstration' of how a correct connection can be made between faith and liberating action. Unlike liberation theology, which 'begins with the poor and arrives at Christ,' Aparecida 'begins with Christ and arrives at the poor,' clearly establishing that 'the Christ-principle always includes the poor, but the poor-principle does not necessarily include Christ ... The original source of theology is nothing other than faith in Christ.' (Magister, 2008)

Magister continues:

> In his brother's view, the thesis of Clodovis should be reversed: 'It is not true that liberation theology replaces God and Christ with the poor ... It was Christ who wanted to identify himself with the poor. The place of the poor is a privileged place of encounter with the Lord. Those who encounter the poor inevitably encounter Christ, still in his crucified form, asking to be taken down from the cross and brought back to life.'

As for the consequences of the attack made by Clodovis against liberation theology, Leonardo Boff writes:

> My suspicion is that the criticisms advanced by Clodovis provide the local and Roman ecclesiastical authorities with the weapons they need to condemn it again, and, who knows, maybe outlaw it definitively from the ecclesial sphere.

I have quoted this article at length because it provides an illustration of three key points. First, it raises the question of the sources of theology. This is not simply – though it is this – a question of whether we start with the poor or with Christ; it is a question of where Christ is to be found. So even though they are agreed that we start with Christ, they are not agreed where that place is. Leonardo thinks it is in the poor; Clodovis thinks it is in faith.

Second, it indicates that even within a specific tradition and place and even family (two brothers in Latin America, both Catholic and both liberation theologians), fundamental differences of understanding concerning the sources of theology may occur. Third, this material indicates that theological judgements are also ecclesial and political – Leonardo locates Clodovis' public pronouncements within an ongoing battle about liberation theology in the Catholic Church.

In this debate we may ask ourselves, Who is trusting what and why? Who is suspicious of what and why?

## The 'masters of suspicion'

During a pastoral theology seminar I invited the participants to comment on various features of the Enlightenment and how theology had responded to these. We talked about the so-called 'masters of suspicion' – Marx, Nietzsche and Freud – and about the political, philosophical and psychological critiques of religion associated with these names and with the Enlightenment more generally. An Eastern Orthodox participant said: 'then how will you dialogue with us, for whom these things haven't happened?' He then added that Marx had certainly happened to them, but not in a positive way; Marx represented for them the regimes that had martyred their bishops.

This incident points up several issues. First, that not all people of the same faith share the same cultural history. That cultural history affects how people feel about things, how they think and thus how they do their theology. Second, this opens up a range of issues about how theology is related to the human sciences and indeed beyond that to other disciplines – in science, the arts or philosophy. Many Orthodox would not only be uncomfortable with a positive reading of the Marxist critique of religion and sociological perspectives associated with it, but also with the assumptions and procedures of western psychology (Jillions, 2003). This suspicion is indeed also shared in differing measure by Christians of other ecclesial traditions.

For some people of faith the opening up of the possibility of critiquing the authorities in our tradition from other disciplines brings life. It allows us to hold on to faith in a fresh way, one that is consistent with our changing understandings and does not sidestep thorny questions that have arisen for us. A good example of this is how the questions opened by feminist perspectives on traditional Christian theology have enabled some women to find new understandings and expressions of faith. For others such critique calls into question the rich life and the experience of God that comes to us through trustful inhabiting of our tradition and its authorities.

The critical awareness required in a master's degree does not require of us any specific cultural history, nor does it rule out the trustful inhabiting of a tradition. What is important is to be able to reflect on and articulate clearly what we trust and why, of what we are suspicious and why. For example, what is our view of the Bible and why do we hold it? How does this affect how we do our theology and how we interrogate human experience? Articulating this indicates in itself a thoughtful and critical analysis and evaluation. It allows us to adopt a position of looking at ourselves and our context, of seeking to understand where we are and why we are there, and to give a good account of this.

# Critique or interpretation?

The very terms 'critique' and 'critical' suggest for many a negative and inappropriate stance towards the authoritative sources of faith and theology. I have found in teaching that common ground is more easily found in the idea of 'interpretation'. Interpretation is a key concept in theology. We interpret texts, we interpret teachings. Those texts and teachings themselves came into being as people attempted to interpret events around them and what God was doing in the world. The Christian doctrine of the Holy Spirit, as guide and teacher who leads into truth, indicates a role for human understanding and interpretation in the work of theology.

Setting out not only our own interpretation but also the grounds on which we make it gives evidence of that kind of critical analysis looked for by the learning outcomes of theology master's courses. Furthermore, it is helpful to look at those interpretations that challenge our own – even if only to explain why we want to stick with our original understanding. But sometimes our understanding grows, and it is good to state in assignments the ways studying this particular material or module has either faced us with challenges or even enabled us to grow and develop in our thinking.

One strategy used in a critical approach to theology, to its texts and teachings, is known as the 'hermeneutics of suspicion'. Such an approach seeks to unearth underlying ideological commitments and expose them, especially drawing attention to the effects of power dynamics in the production of theology. Various forms of liberation theology draw on this strategy. There is much that is valuable in this approach, in helping us to understand better the realities of how texts and practices are produced.

However, challenges do not always come from direct suspicion and negativity about our original position. There are other models to work with. One is to use comparison and analogy – engaging with a different perspective in order to see what we didn't see before. This analogical or comparative way of gaining a critical space and of being dialectical is a more fruitful and nuanced alternative to the 'debunking' inherent in strong versions of a 'hermeneutic of suspicion', and partners well an attention to reflexivity. It may help you to see both the strengths and weaknesses of your initial view-point. Learning in a context where others are of different church traditions, different faiths or no faith, offers possibilities for this: 'I really enjoyed the ecumenical aspects of the course – sharing a seminar with people from other traditions and contexts. This created a tension that was implicit in the learning process that was both challenging and exciting' (Emma, a student on our Pastoral Theology MA).

A good bibliography also helps, one that uses not only books from your own tradition or viewpoint but expands your horizons beyond this and challenges it. Always check your bibliography to be sure it includes a variety of perspectives. If you do not know the perspective the material is coming from, then that is an important thing to find out – you need to contextualize your sources and explain the background and position of the author in order to be able to use a source properly at master's level.

The Bible is a particularly difficult text to interpret and use well in theology, and master's students often struggle, caught between a sense that theology must be seriously connected to the Bible and an inability to see how to relate the text of Scripture to the text of today. I have written extensively about this elsewhere (Bennett, 2013), and have suggested in the References and Further Resources

section below some other books you might find helpful in exploring this more deeply (Ford and Stanton, 2003; Riches, 2000). One
way to help yourself identify your own position and to be self-
critical about using the Bible is to look at a typology[1] of different
ways the Bible is used and interpreted. A helpful one can be found
in Roger Walton's article, 'Using the Bible and Christian tradition
in theological reflection' in *The British Journal of Theological
Education* (Walton, 2003). This looks at how students themselves
in the institutions where Walton taught actually did use the Bible
in engaging with issues. He lists: links and associations, proof-
texting, resonance and analogy, exploring a theological theme, an
extrapolated question to take to the tradition, a one-way critique
and a mutual critique between the Bible and experience. You may
well feel the typology is inadequate – all the better if you can be
critical of it. But it could be a useful heuristic device for examining
your own position and use of the Bible.

# Finding a critical space

Balancing commitment and critique is a tricky business. In studying theology in higher education we often find ourselves torn
between these two poles. Are we 'insiders' or 'outsiders'? Are we
looking at issues from a position of faith and of involvement? How
do we also and indeed at the same time, since we never cease to
be insiders, look at things with some sense of 'objectivity', of being
able to stand outside or perhaps to stand back a little?

Robert Orsi beautifully encapsulates the dilemma of the religious anthropologist who is both an insider and an outsider in a

---

1 A typology in this sense is a grouping together of approaches that share
similar characteristics. People may cross 'types' – no one person fits one type
perfectly, but looking at the typology helps clarify where you stand.

revealing pair of images. The insider/outsider anthropologist does not, he writes, go 'behind the curtain like Toto in Oz to uncloak the imposter' but rather is like 'a child glancing over his folded hands at his mother at prayer beside him' (2005, p. 160). We may be implicated in what we study; it may have the emotional reson-ance for us of our mother at prayer – such feelings and such a personal history may well go right back to childhood. In Orsi's image we can observe our mother praying with a certain distance and from outside. But our knowledge is from the perspective of one who is also praying and who is related to the one we observe. Furthermore, our observation is intimate and empathetic.

Commitment may, as in the image I have just explored, be a longstanding involvement in a set of practices of faith. On the other hand, it may take the form of a new way of looking at things, which we have just discovered and for which we are fervent advo-cates. An example of this would be people who had recently discovered that the perspective offered by Black theology enabled them to make sense of their experience in the Church. Under these circumstances we tend to adopt an 'advocacy' stance. Such a posi-tion may *feel* critical to us – as it may be very critical of traditional theology and practice – but in fact it neglects to look critically at the things we are advocating. Always ask yourself the questions: How might someone else critique the position I am taking? What are the challenges to it from those who think differently? How might I myself be critical of my own position? All of this raises your critical thinking to what is expected at master's level.

I would like to finish this discussion of critique and commitment with a personal story. When I first began working at postgraduate level in theology, I came to my studies with a strong Christian faith of an open evangelical kind. I was asking questions that had been provoked by my life experience and by some intellectual knotty problems I had encountered. My 'critical space' was the Cambridge

University Library. There I would hide away from my family and my domestic duties and read. I would read bits of a book or an article and, provoked by what I was reading, get the next book or article mentioned in the bibliography. I guess many people today use the internet in this way – to move on from one set of ideas to the next and, crucially, from one *question* to the next. This is how we learn, moving onward and upward or sometimes round and round, allowing our own questions to lead us on. One day I found I was feeling very anxious, even frightened. My questions were leading me into deep water in which I could not swim but might drown. I called it a day. I didn't give up my studies, but I decided I had pursued that particular question as far as it was going – for the time being. I came back to it later. I tell this story because it is so important that we find a place within the dialectic of commitment and critique that is good enough for the expectations laid on us by master's level study but enables us to flourish, not drown.

# 7

# Especially for International Students

At home we write fewer essays and have more oral exams ... I didn't spend so much time in libraries ... there were text books for every course ... How do UK students do it? (Bennett Moore, Faltin and Wright, 2003, p. 72)

## Some strange British habits

International students arriving in Britain to do a master's course encounter a great deal of culture shock. Yours will vary depending where you have come from – North or South America, China, Russia, Germany, Africa, Australia – but there will always be culture shock. Some strange British habits are not directly to do with your studies. Students I have worked with regularly identify things ranging from separate hot and cold taps to the British habit of saying 'you must come for a meal' then never offering a specific invitation. The habits I will concentrate on here, however, are academic ones related to master's studies.

The first of these you may notice is the question of what to call your tutors. Ahdaf Soueif, in her partly autobiographical novel *In the Eye of the Sun*, tells of Asya, who travels from Cairo to a cold and wet university in the north of England for postgraduate study. She meets her supervisor for the first time and addresses him as 'Professor'.

> 'Ah! – you mustn't call me Professor you know.' He gives her a quick, shy smile. 'You can call me Bill.'
> 'Oh! Right. Thank you.'
> Of course, she can't possibly call him 'Bill'. But now she can't call him anything else either. (Soueif, 1992, p. 330)

Tutors should of course be sensitive to this, but if they are not, do try and discuss it with them or with fellow students, rather than feel embarrassed and silenced.

A second thing that may shock you initially, as it did the student in our research quoted at the beginning of this chapter, is just how much private study time you have and how free you are to organize you own study – to decide what to read, indeed to find it for yourself and to direct your own learning. You may expect to have large amounts of class time, to be offered set reading handed out in photocopies and to be given quite specific things to learn for the next class, on which you may be tested. Instead you find yourself handed a reading list, inducted into how to find more material via internet searches through a library system whose technology defeats you, and left to your own devices. The British students may think this is quite normal, and tutors may think they have given you plenty of guidance. You may therefore feel awkward about raising the fact that this way of doing things is all new to you. I encourage you again to raise this with the tutors concerned. They will normally be more than happy to give some time to helping you work out how to get the best out of your study time. You may also find there are specific sessions arranged in your university for international students, either directly relating to study skills or perhaps more social, where you can share these issues with others in a similar position.

# Critical thinking

Critical thinking is a value highly prized in UK higher education, but what does this concept mean, and might there be different expectations of its meaning in the UK from those held elsewhere? Skills and attitudes commonly associated with critical thinking are the ability to identify how arguments work, evaluate assumptions, clarify ideas and see things in context. Critical thinking implies making judgements.

This, however, is not the end of the matter. In many educational contexts, critical thinking is text-based and analytical. You are expected to look at a specific text closely and to be able to pull the argument apart, consider its component parts and perhaps comment on it. In a UK context all this is important, but more emphasis is put on the personally reflective, creative and constructive elements in critical thinking. Put simply, high marks are given to those who display flair, imagination, independence of thought and their own judgement (suitably evidenced and supported by argument). This has its downside: sometimes students in the UK build some high-flown arguments with very little infrastructure. But the key thing to grasp is that analysing the views of authorities/ texts is only half of what is expected. These authorities and texts are 'conversation partners' for you to use to examine and indeed critique your own argument. This can feel a very strange task to be doing at master's level.

Here is a basic framework with which you might work:

- Analyse the question that has been set and decide what your initial ideas on how to answer it might be – this helps put your ideas up front in the driving seat.
- Identify some reading from a variety of perspectives, ideally including recently published material, that will help you develop and expand and indeed challenge your initial ideas.
- Make notes on that reading, identifying how each piece is useful – or not – to what you want to say.
- Make a plan of your answer, showing each step and what sources you will use to discuss each of these. Remember to use material that challenges you as well as material that supports you.
- Write the essay! Have a short and clear conclusion saying where you have got to, not introducing new material.[1]

## That dreaded seminar

People from the UK are more comfortable in seminars. They can waffle; it's more difficult to sustain fifteen minutes for those who have just to go straight to the point. (Bennett Moore, Faltin and Wright, 2003, p. 81)

Some English people have a problem in that they can't ask a question – it turns into a speech. People listen politely in England when this happens! (p. 86)

These two remarks by students indicate some of the problems international students may encounter in seminars. The first is related to language issues. If English is not your first language, then you have

---

1 For further help in doing this, see Stott et al., 2000.

to overcome all sorts of barriers to speak in a seminar, whether you are the student presenting or just a member of the group. Obvious problems relate to whether you can find the words quickly or whether others in the group are able to understand the accent in which you speak English. Then there is the need to understand how the discussion is going – unlike when reading, you can't go back over the words slowly. The student I quoted identifies something less obvious – the way first speakers of a language can just pad things out. All of this contributes to a lack of comfort and possibly to a fear of taking part in seminars.

Some possible ways to overcome this might be:

- to prepare well for a seminar and to write down some points you might want to make in advance;
- if you are giving the paper, to practise with a friend first and ask her or him to comment on your clarity of speaking, your speed and volume and other aspects of your presentation in advance;
- to discuss with the tutor your difficulties and look together for ways to maximize your contribution in that particular context.

The second student's comment above is more general and suggests that expectations of how contributions will be made in a seminar vary culturally. This student clearly expected a culture of precise questions and succinct answers – perhaps also one in which if people didn't adhere to this, other students would complain. At the opposite end of the scale, some cultures would expect people to contribute and talk at great length, to share stories and talk all around a topic. It might be considered extremely rude to cut them short or interrupt. It is helpful to discuss in the group the expectations of how contributions will be made in seminars. If tutors don't do this, perhaps you might ask them to. It will be of benefit to all the students, not just to the international students.

There is one more issue some international students encounter in a seminar context. The mindset and assumptions of others in the group may be so foreign to your own that you feel there is no place from which to make your contribution that the others would understand. It is as if, in more than a strictly literal sense, they are 'talking another language'. There would be too many things that would need to be explained first. This is a difficulty for which there are some solutions in terms of the overall life of the group, but one which is probably most easily tackled by talking first with the tutor.

# English-language issues

Most universities have a minimum language requirement for candidates whose first language is not English. Even though you meet this requirement, you may find yourself struggling. It may well be that your university offers free language support, usually in groups or classes. If so, it is helpful to take advantage of these.

Language issues do not just cause difficulties in seminars. They may impede your understanding of books and articles and also of lectures, especially if the lecturer goes fast or has an accent of any kind that you find difficult to understand. Try asking if you might record the lectures, or ask for text or notes to be made available to you.

Coping with assessment tasks is also made more difficult if you are not working in your first language. You may find that you need longer to complete tasks. You may also find that the word lengths do not seem adequate to express yourself in a language that is not you own natural one. It is not possible to have different rules for different students, but universities normally put in place systems of support – language and other study skills – for those who are struggling. It is always good to ask someone else – someone who speaks English as a first language – to read over your work and to suggest where you have incorrect English or where your meaning is not clear.

# Canon versus context

When you come to study theology as an international student you are uprooted from your context and thrown into a new one. As a student in the UK you will find, whichever area of theology you are studying, that there is a 'canon' of authors and thinkers in that area that will appear on reading lists, be mentioned in lectures and with which you will be expected to be familiar. Such a canon or classic body of thinking will probably be western and may well be culture-specific to Western Europe and/or North America. Of course, this is not always the case, and some courses and modules are honourable exceptions. Nevertheless, you may find yourself in the canon-versus-context dilemma: studying in the UK, how much weight do you give to the texts normally used in that context, and how much to those used in your own? Can you indeed find the material that relates to your own context?

This can raise particular issues if you are doing a course in practical theology in which you are required to research a context. Do you choose your own context? If so, how do you access information and materials relating to it?

There are no easy answers to these questions. The crucial thing is that you are aware of them and if necessary bring them to the attention of your tutor. In your actual assignments you could explore the difficulties of working from one context (your own) while much of the theoretical literature comes from a different context (the place where you are studying). This would demonstrate critical awareness of the issues and enhance your work greatly.

## Assessment

Different educational systems have different expectations in respect of assessment tasks. United Kingdom master's degrees in theology normally work with essays of around 5,000–8,000 words for each module and a dissertation of around 15,000 words. Of course, this varies enormously, and the requirement for essays is often supplemented by assessed seminar presentations and sometimes by book reviews, learning journals, placement reports or even group projects. The system you come from may use exams, short in-class tests and regular short papers to submit. You may be used to being given a page length, not a word length, for your paper or even to writing freely with no maximum length.

One specific thing it is good to recognize is that the educational system in the UK puts a high premium on answering the set question in an essay. An essay title is not just a springboard from which you can write around that topic in any way you want. I have seen this expectation catch out students time and time again – especially students from the USA. The examiners are looking for a well-argued answer to the question set. They are looking for various and differing points of view on the question, informed by your reading, and then they are looking for how you yourself build up an argument to answer the question.

A crucial 'strange British habit' is the absolute requirement not to plagiarize (see Chapters 2 and 5). International students are particularly vulnerable to the possibility of plagiarizing without meaning to commit an offence. There are many reasons for this. Some revolve around the strict expectation in the UK of the use of quotation marks for *everything* that is quoted word for word from a source. A further difficulty is that in many educational systems courses are chosen by students because they wish to learn the thinking of a particular professor, and assessment tasks consist in reproducing carefully the thought of that professor. This can easily lead to plagiarism. Finally, there are issues around 'voice' in plagiarism. In some cultures there are authorities that have a public voice – professors, church leaders, a particular political party, colonial or missionary legacies – and it is not considered appropriate for a 'lowly' student to use their own voice. This also can lead to plagiarism as you may be nervous of speaking for yourself and may not be used to doing so.

## In conclusion

To have students and indeed staff who bring an international dimension is vital to master's courses in theology in the UK. Such a dimension combats insularity and closed-mindedness and opens up fresh thinking and new perspectives. As an international student you enhance the quality of the learning experience for all. But being an international student is not always easy and raises particular issues for study skills. I hope that this chapter has named some of these and suggested helpful ways forward. It is only a start, and I urge you to look at the suggested further resources at the end of this book and at what your own university offers by way of face-to-face classes or on its website.

# 8

# Doing your Dissertation

## What do I want to research?

### Choosing a topic

Writing a dissertation on a topic of your own choice is an exciting and a daunting prospect. You may well have identified an area you would like to work in before you started your MA. This is good, but one thing is really important. A senior colleague of mine once wisely said to me: 'If you want to say something, write a book; if you want to find something out, do a PhD'. For 'PhD' he could have substituted 'master's dissertation'. His point was that doing any kind of academic postgraduate research is not about parading our hobby horse, getting a chance to have our say on something we believe passionately; it is about doing a piece of research to find out something we didn't know before and then writing up that research carefully – and telling what we have found out. So the key question is, What do you want to find out?

For a master's degree, unlike a doctorate, you do not have to make an original contribution to knowledge. But you do have to research something for yourself and make fresh connections, offer a new approach or engage your own experience with a theoretical perspective. A master's dissertation is not just a very long essay;

even less is it three short ones stuck together. It is a report of work you have done to research a topic independently, and the building of that work into an argument you want to make on the subject. I hope this chapter will help you see something of the character and shape of what is required.

You may be someone who is more daunted than excited, and feels stuck at the first hurdle, with no idea of what topic to work on for your dissertation. Here are some possible questions to ask yourself that might help you:

- What am I interested in?
- What specific expertise am I bringing?
- Which topics on the course have especially engaged my interest, and that I might like to take further?
- Is there a question that arises from my practice or experience?
- Is there an area in which there is a gap in knowledge, to which I might make a contribution?

Don't choose something too big. In 18 years of directing an MA, I can honestly say that never have I been presented a dissertation proposal that was too small – many times I have received proposals that would have required two or three PhDs. Everyone is terrified they won't be able to write enough words. So they pile on topics: a chapter here on the history of biblical interpretation of the topic, then one on the history of the topic from St Paul to the twenty-first century, and then a survey of what 100 people in three local congregations think about the topic – and we are still only halfway through. It is just far too much to explore in any depth at all.

One of the difficulties about a master's dissertation is to pitch it correctly – it is not an undergraduate dissertation, nor is it a doctorate. You *are required*:

- to work and think independently;
- to offer something fresh and not just a regurgitation of secondary material;
- to manage a large body of material and present it in an ordered way;
- to look in depth at some area of your academic field, including relevant primary or secondary literature;
- to address ethics issues appropriately;
- to display a sound, but not necessarily comprehensive, understanding of any discipline you draw on (this is particularly important where you are being interdisciplinary – for example, drawing on New Testament studies in a practical theology dissertation).

You are *not required* to have an in-depth knowledge of all recent literature in the area of your study, write 80,000–100,000 words, offer an original contribution to knowledge or conduct empirical research that would take two years to process. These are often features of PhDs, but *not* of master's dissertations.

## Are there appropriate resources?

Choosing a topic to research may have some constraints. Is there an available supervisor? This is a key question. Supervisors are appointed by the university, normally through the programme director, and are usually members of staff of the institution, though they may be external. It is more important to have a supervisor who knows what is required of a master's dissertation and how to help you achieve that than it is to have a supervisor who is an expert in the field. You can do your own literature search, and you can usually arrange a one-off consultation with an expert.

However, if your topic needs specialist guidance that is unavailable, then you simply cannot pursue it. Furthermore, a potential supervisor may have good advice in framing a topic. So this is an iterative process, back and forth between your ideas for your topic and available supervision and expert guidance.

Here is an equally crucial question: Is your research question answerable? I have seen some unanswerable ones in my time. For example, 'What are the motives behind those who hijack aeroplanes?' foundered on the difficulties of conducting the necessary interviews to answer the question. 'What does God think of contemporary methods of mission such as Fresh Expressions?' encountered similar difficulties! Again we have an iterative process – identify a question, ask how it could be answered and modify the question in the light of difficulties. Thus the latter question could become an evaluation of Fresh Expressions from a particular theological stance.

You should also ask whether there are the resources to answer your question in the context in which you will be doing the work. Where are the key books and articles on this topic? Is there primary material in some specialist library and is it near enough to visit? Where and who are the people you might need to interview, and are they available and willing? Will you have to travel and will this cost money? If you are an international student, are the resources you need located in the place where you will do the research? Again, consideration of all this may cause you to modify your question.

Finally, you might like to consider whether the topic you have chosen might either have too much or too little by way of sources to draw on. If your topic is awash with secondary literature, you may find yourself unable to find a new angle specific to yourself, and may end up writing a general essay on the topic. On the other hand, if there is very little material you may feel that the task of relating your question to a wider debate is too demanding for a master's dissertation. As you search for literature, don't forget that non-academic sources, such as church reports, may offer a rich resource.

## Finding a conceptual framework

A colleague of mine (in English studies) was confronted by a student dressed in black with black-dyed hair who said, 'I am going to do my dissertation on vampires!' 'Why?', asked my colleague. 'Because I am a Goth, and I am very interested in vampires.' 'What particular aspect of vampires?' 'Uh?' 'What do you want to find out about vampires?' 'Oh, *everything*!' They eventually settled on vampires in Victorian literature.

When you have settled on a topic, you need to think through the aspect from which you will approach it. Imagine a photograph of a cake – a nice luscious creamy cake. There are many aspects from which you might do a dissertation on this cake – and with those aspects go specific academic disciplines: the history of cake-making in England (history, domestic history in particular); the role of food in celebrations (sociology?); dieting (could be medicine or psychology); food pornography (feminist studies); cakes and rituals (sociology, religious studies).

Within theology you might be interested in pilgrimage. Would this be the history of pilgrimage? Pilgrimage as a practice for parishes? Biblical understandings of pilgrimage? The theology of place and space? You need to choose what conceptual framework you are coming from. What is the aspect of pilgrimage that most interests you? What kind of literature will you be reading to illuminate this? Choosing your framework in this way narrows down your work and enables you to begin focusing in depth. It helps you select what to include and what to exclude. It gives you a framework in which to research and to make an argument.

It is important that your conceptual framework is appropriate to the framework of the MA you are enrolled on. For example, we have two theology MAs in the institution for which I work. One is an MA in Pastoral Theology. In this I would expect that students examine a topic using a conceptual framework that involves reflection on practice. So to take our example of pilgrimage: the practices of parishes is obviously appropriate; history or biblical understandings or the theology of place and space would be secondary, perhaps underpinning or illuminating the primary framework. In our other MA, in Christian Theology, the students study at least two of either biblical studies, doctrine or missiology. They then look at overarching issues of theological method by relating these disciplines to each other in relation to a topic. So if one of them were to choose pilgrimage, they might choose to look at it as a means of mission in relation to biblical understandings of pilgrimage. I will leave it to your imagination to work out how students on each of these programmes might study cakes or vampires.

## Ethics issues

All universities now, rightly, have a code of ethics for researchers and expectations of procedures with regard to obtaining permission to do research with human or animal subjects. These apply to all staff and students, and it is absolutely inappropriate to conduct even one interview for your research without going through the procedures and getting permission.

The ethics procedures themselves will give you guidance in what is required, and this will differ from one university to the next.

However, there are two issues to which everyone needs to attend. The first is whether actually doing the research you propose to do is ethical in itself. Do you have the necessary expertise? Are you disturbing people, especially on sensitive topics, for a good enough reason? Furthermore, are there any issues for yourself, such as that the answers may not be manageable for you either in terms of volume or of emotional content?

The second issue is about timing. Ethics procedures in universities can take time, and you may not have much of that. It is better not to embark on something that requires a more complex procedure of permission, such as working with children, vulnerable adults or very delicate issues. Anyone working in the NHS or the Prison Service should note that there are ethics procedures particular to those institutions that may take a very long time to process.

# How am I going to conduct my research?

## Forming a proposal

You will probably be asked to submit a proposal for your dissertation, and there may be a specific form in which your university requires this. In order to make a viable proposal you will need to think through a logical sequence of questions: What do I want to find out? How might I find that out? What resources will I need? How will I write it up? It is much better to think this way than to start with the question: What will my content/chapter headings be? You cannot know your content until you have answered these questions.

Here is a mock proposal that we use in the Cambridge Theological Federation. This is not a blueprint, just a suggestion of how a proposal might be done.

---

## Mock Dissertation Proposal

[This proposal is based on Gordon Lynch and David Willows, *Telling Tales: The Narrative Dimension of Pastoral Care and Counselling*, Contact Pastoral Monograph Number 8, 1998. I have constructed what a dissertation proposal might look like if the end result was to be this monograph! All actual quotations from Lynch and Willows are in quotation marks.]

**Name:**
**Title:** 'Telling tales: The narrative dimension of pastoral care and counselling'
**SID number:**

### Area of research

'Over the past 30 years there has been a growing ... awareness of the crucial role that stories play in human interaction and the generation of knowledge.' This is reflected in 'the trend towards narrative-based studies, both in the humanities and in the human sciences'. The aim of this dissertation is to explore 'concepts and issues relating to narrative', which are 'significant ... for the practice of pastoral care and counselling'. This exploration will highlight 'the narrative dimension of pastoral theology and of pastoral care and counselling' and will consider the relevance of this narrative dimension to pastoral practice.

## Proposed methodology and structure

Because 'one of the dangers of writing about narrative ... is that it can quickly turn into a highly abstract or theoretical discussion' I propose to use two stories from my own experience as the starting point for reflection. I shall explore the 'particular functions that stories and story-telling can have for us' in the light of the telling of these particular stories. I shall further explore, still in dialogue with my original narratives, theological issues that arise in connection with the understanding of our stories in relation to stories from Scripture and religious tradition, in particular those of the Christian tradition. Finally, I propose to examine the 'relevance of narrative thinking to ... pastoral care and counselling'.

1. Introduction
To include:
- my reasons for considering the topic to be of significance;
- brief highlighting of recent literature with which I will be engaging;
- scope of what is covered in the dissertation;
- how my material will be ordered and why.

2. 'A narrative beginning'
Narration of the two stories that will form the basis of my reflection. These stories will concern serious issues of life and death; one will probably concern an incident in my personal family life and the other a series of incidents in my pastoral ministry.

3. 'The nature and functions of stories and story-telling'
In this section I will 'reflect upon these personal experiences and ... comment on the particular functions that stories and story-telling can have for us'. I will 'focus on the nature of narrative', examining its 'hermeneutical function in help-ing us to make sense of raw experience'. I will contrast two different views of the function of narrative – 'a view which sees story as a way of defending ourselves against the inher-ent meaninglessness of life' (see Cupitt, 1991) 'and a view which sees story as a way of uncovering the ultimate truths of human existence' (see Frankl, 1964). I will look at the 'provisional and imperfect nature' of the stories we tell – identifying ambiguity and complexity in relation to personal identity, interpersonal relationships, social context and lan-guage. The story-telling of groups will be considered as well as that of individuals.

4. 'Finding ourselves in God's story'
In this section I shall raise questions 'about the continuing relevance of sacred stories in modern society', developing an 'explicitly theological' approach to the question of the nature and function of stories and story-telling. Building on the work of Gerald Loughlin in *Telling God's Story: Bible, Church and Narrative Theology*, and always in dialogue with the stories in Section 2, I shall consider the relationship between the 'stories of our personal experience' and the 'authoritative narratives of our faith tradition'. I shall consider critically the possibility that 'the structure of existence that is pre-sent in the biblical narrative interposes meaning upon my experience and helps me locate myself in relation to some transcendent reality'.

5. 'Rediscovering the narrative dimension of pastoral care and counselling'
In this section I shall develop an account of 'the insights of narrative thinking upon pastoral practice' in the light of the discussion in the dissertation thus far. I shall consider implications for:

- 'new ways of understanding pastoral interaction as the facilitation of open and truthful story-telling';
- 'ethics' – the relationship between the telling of stories and an understanding of 'right action' for communities and for individuals;
- 'mission and proclamation' – 'the story *is* the truth, and the pastoral task is faithfully to narrate this story to the world';
- 'Christian education' – 'a critical dialogue between the Christian Story and our individual stories', taking account of those whose stories are often ignored;
- 'liturgy' – with particular reference to the Eucharist.

6. Conclusion
Summary of the point that has been reached in the dissertation, indication of the main points that emerge from it and suggestion of further questions that are left open-ended and are pointers for future work.

**Initial bibliography**

D. Cupitt, *What is a Story?*, SCM Press, 1991.
V. Frankl, *Man's Search for Meaning*, Penguin, 1964.
K. Gergen, *Realities and Relationship*, Harvard University Press, 1994.

C. Gerkin, *The Living Human Document: Re-Visioning Pastoral Counselling in a Hermeneutical Mode*, Abingdon Press, 1984.

G. Loughlin, *Telling God's Story: Bible, Church and Narrative Theology*, Cambridge University Press, 1996.

T. Sabin, *Narrative Psychology: The Storied Nature of Human Conduct*, Praeger, 1986.

G. W. Stroup, *The Promise of Narrative Theology*, SCM Press, 1981.

### Ethics clearance

If your research involves human or animal subjects, you need Ethics clearance from the University.

Please tick whichever is appropriate.

I have consulted the Ethics Review Check List and:

☐  My research does not involve human or animal subjects.

☐  I have completed the necessary ethics forms and return them with my proposal.

### Proposed supervisor

Dr Carol Singer, 3 Christmas Croft, Toytown, Snowshire
Tel. 76895 99999
Carol.singer@gmail.com

### Cost

It is not envisaged that this dissertation will involve any specific research costs.

Note that the proposal starts with the area of research, and within this opening section it is possible to identify the key research question. It then goes on to address the proposed methodology and structure of the work. If this were an empirical research project there would be other issues to consider about the methods used and how data will be collected and analysed, but the methodology by which you investigate the question is important to address in all dissertations, whether empirical or not.

Note how the proposal shows how each chapter follows from the previous one. Students have objected that it was easy to show this here, as I was basing the proposal on research already done, whereas how can we know how our argument will flow until we have done the research? There is some truth in this. However, you do need to know how you propose to develop an argument, not just dump in a load of information. It is perhaps the headings of these chapters that indicate a sense that the authors know how they will develop their work – starting from locating their work in the theoretical perspective of the nature and function of story-telling (that's the view they will take of this 'cake'), narrowing down to a theological perspective on this matter and indeed to a particularly significant contribution in this area by Loughlin, then looking at the particular relevance of this for their own area of interest, pastoral care and counselling. This can perfectly well be thought through, and indeed should be, before undertaking the dissertation work.

Note also how the proposal is clear about the methodology: the author will start by narrating two stories and work from that to theoretical considerations. This is a dissertation in pastoral/practical theology and it employs a methodology of reflection on practice appropriate to that discipline.

Some key secondary literature is proposed and referenced in the proposal, to show how this dissertation will be anchored in a wider discussion and established theoretical perspectives.

If I were to revise this mock proposal I would add a word count to each proposed chapter; there is nothing like a word count to show up how much you are trying to cover. This will also serve you well as you start to write, holding you back from writing too much and then having to cut masses out.

## How can my question be answered?

It may be that the question you have asked can be answered in large part or in whole through theoretical considerations, which demand the reading of books and articles, using primary or secondary sources. Suppose you were looking at what John Ruskin's annotations on his personal Bibles could contribute to an understanding of biblical hermeneutics in practical theology (my own research). You would definitely need to look at Ruskin's annotations and at Ruskin's own writings (primary sources); but you would also need to use some secondary sources – on biblical interpretation in the Victorian era, on Ruskin's life and on current debates in biblical hermeneutics in practical theology. I would argue that this question cannot be fully addressed without also some consideration of the practices of our contemporaries in biblical interpretation, which you might access through reflection on practice or through some empirical research. But you might decide that this is too much for one master's dissertation, and you would specifically state in your proposal that you are addressing certain particular aspects of the question.

I have now named the four most likely sources of information for a master's dissertation in theology:

- primary or documentary sources;
- secondary literature giving contextual information and/or theoretical perspectives;

- reflection on our own practice or on that we have encountered;
- empirical research such as interviews, questionnaires, focus groups, case studies and observations.

Many dissertations will mix these.

Empirical research, conducted using the methods of the social sciences, often though not always inductive and qualitative in nature, is becoming increasingly used in pastoral/practical theology. How to do this properly is the subject of a book in its own right, and two books that are really helpful for starters are Bell's *Doing Your Research Project* (2010) and Swinton's and Mowat's *Practical Theology and Qualitative Research* (2006). Another text many students find useful is Robson's *Real World Research* (2011). I have listed all of these in the References and Further Resources section. Many master's programmes offer credit-bearing modules or extra research training that specifically address the conduct of empirical research in theology, and my advice would be not even to consider doing this kind of research unless you have received training in it. The chances of your doing it well if you haven't received training are minimal.

There are myriad ways of approaching a question in a theology master's dissertation, and consultation with your supervisor or module leader is vital. Here are some I have seen bear good fruit.

- Start with a question that arises from your practice or experience; analyse the issue then draw in key voices from the literature on the topic to engage with your questions and develop your understanding. (This is very close to the method used in the mock proposal.)
- Use a comparison to set up a problem, for example comparing the approaches of theologian x and theologian y to an issue in order to understand its complexities better, or contrasting the approaches within two different ecclesial traditions.

- Convene a focus group to make an initial exploration of an issue, which will generate perspectives you may not have thought about and allow you to identify specific issues to follow up in your research.
- Use a published method of theological reflection (see Chapter 4, pp. 65–66) to work through an issue.

## In what form will I present my research?

There are three main forms in which a master's dissertation in theology is likely to be submitted: a traditional discursive essay format; a social sciences style research report; an alternative 'creative' piece of work.

- **Traditional format** This is the form envisaged in the mock proposal. It is in many ways the easiest form as it is well tried and tested in theology, and is a form you have probably used in a shorter version many times over. But that in a way is the catch. It is tempting to make your dissertation just a longer essay or some shorter essays stitched together. A friend who is a priest in the Anglican Church in Wales was invited by the local Baptist minister to preach. He said, 'We normally preach for 40 minutes.' When my friend protested that she couldn't possibly write a sermon that went on longer than 20 minutes, he said. 'Well, don't you have two sermons you could bring and preach one after the other?' A 15,000-word dissertation is not two 7,500-word essays 'preached one after the other'. What I have said in the previous section about answering a research question and about forming a proposal should help you avoid this.
- **Social science format** Research reports in the social sciences generally take a standard form: establishment of research ques-

tion; literature review; methodology and methods; findings; discussion of findings. This can be a helpful framework if you are doing empirical research. However, theology, even practical theology, is not straightforwardly a social science. While this format is there for you to draw from, there may be other elements expected in your dissertation, or perhaps empirical research is just one part of what you are doing. Expectations in this matter differ in different contexts and universities, and you should discuss this with your tutor or supervisor and be very clear what is expected.

- **Creative format** Some programmes allow for the possibility of candidates offering 'dissertations' in a variety of forms, sometimes called 'major projects'. It may be possible to offer, for example, a piece of film or music, liturgy, artwork or creative writing. I have encountered a performed musical, a photography exhibition and a piano recital as part of major projects – and in the context of other modules, artwork, liturgy and drama. Be adventurous – but also negotiate carefully what you will do. How many written words by way of explanation, evaluation and exploration must accompany your creative offering? How will the creative element be assessed – by what criteria? How does the creative element help to meet the learning outcomes specified for the module? Students working in this way often find that their energies are all taken up in the creative work, and they have little left over for the commentary. Sadly, this often results in a lower mark as the critical element is missing. One way of avoiding this is to keep a research diary from the start, noting and discussing your decisions along the creative journey and reflecting on them – so you will have plenty of material for the commentary that is not 'tired' but richly engaged with your creative project.

# How am I going to write up my research?

## Telling a story

Writing up your research is telling a story. It is a story of:

- what you have done;
- what you have found out;
- how you interpret what you have found out – what you think it means;
- what you think is the significance of what you have found out.

## Conceptualizing

Writing up your research is also a mapping exercise – how do the bits fit together and why? As you plan how to tell the story, think through how you might show the connections between the different elements. This raises the level of your thinking and writing. A diagram often helps to make connections clear, and there are many helpful ones readily available to use. The following figures show three possible ways of showing connections. All these shapes are easily available in SmartArt in Microsoft Word 2010. I have tried to conceptualize my own research under each of these models. Some are more sophisticated than others; some display the features and significance of the work better than others. Different models will suit different kinds of work.

The model in Figure 4 works best for a thesis that starts with a question, proceeds to bring in further information to examine that question and moves logically to a new position on the question.

It is useful in that it indicates how your own argument builds up, how you use your sources and how you have got somewhere at the end that is further on than the beginning.

## Figure 4  Building up the argument

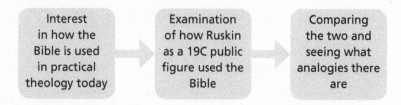

The model in Figure 5 shows the key issue at the centre and, round the edges, the various issues I will consider in order to illuminate the central question. The main issue with which I start is at the top in a position that indicates its key place. This model is less linearly logical than the last, and it indicates a way of addressing an issue from several sides, each side bringing in new material and sources – secondary reading and experience.

## Figure 5  Illuminating the central question

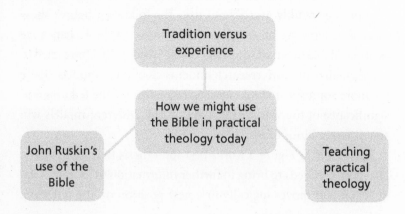

## Figure 6 Making complex interconnections

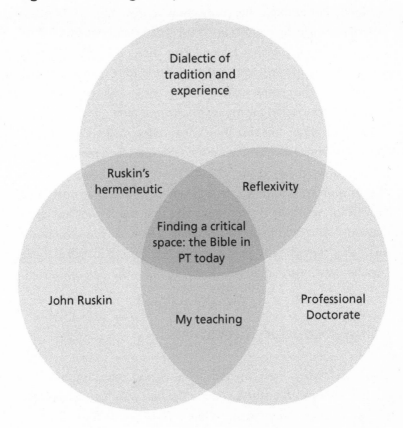

Figure 6 is a classic Venn diagram, extremely useful for showing complex interconnections in your material in a sophisticated way. If you use it, do not forget to fill in all seven sections otherwise the whole point of the connections is missed (you will need to draw text boxes for the inner ones). I have used this diagram to show three levels: on the first level are the three areas from which I have drawn material: the dialectic of tradition and experience; how John Ruskin used the Bible; how the Bible is used in our Professional Doctorate programme. At the next level of intersection I have shown how any two of these yields a further dimension of my thinking – for example, the connection between the tradition and experience dialectic and Ruskin is the understanding of how Ruskin was bringing together his understanding of the Bible and his understanding of contemporary life, what kind of hermeneutic he was using. In the central space I show how these all come together to take me forward in my main research question.

Using diagrams like this shows how different elements of your work are connected – see Figure 1 in Chapter 2 for a further example. It allows you to explain *why* you are bringing in each element of your sources, your reflection and your argument, and how these fit with the whole. It is very important that you do not just drop diagrams in with little or no explanation. Instead you should use them as a springboard for discussion, explaining in words what elements you have included and why, and how they are connected.

## Using secondary literature

This is your work, based on your research and your thinking. You are the author of the story; you are the one who has conceptualized and mapped your work. While it is, of course, essential that you use the work of others to sharpen, inform and challenge your thinking and to offer theoretical perspectives within which to frame your discussion, this work is yours. Four verbs give an indication of how you might treat the work of others as you use it to develop your own:

- Summarize – make sure you have checked out key work that might have been done recently in relation to your research question, and that you mention it. But note: this is only the first step.
- Synthesize – show connections between your sources. Which

came first? Do they contradict or complement each other? How are they related? What are the implications for your work? Pull things together – using perhaps a chronological model of key themes.

- Analyse – look at this work carefully to see whether it is of use to you and why. Evaluate it critically.
- Authorize – take what you need up into your own argument. Take a stand in which you take this body of knowledge further or deliberately take an opposing position.

## Using your supervisor

Last but by no means least, you are not alone in this enterprise. You have a supervisor. Check out what the regulations in your context are for a supervisor's role. How many supervisions will you be offered? Will the supervisor help with the proposal? Will he or she be expected/allowed to check a final draft? My doctor said to me that the silliest thing a person can do with their medicine is not bother to take it. Not bothering to use your supervisor is likewise silly. Used properly from the beginning, your supervisor can help you to achieve a much higher mark than you would get without him or her.

You will need to see your supervisor at the beginning of your project – to set you out on the right track, perhaps indicate some useful resources, agree a timetable of meetings and when work is to be handed in for discussion along the way, and help you see an overall plan. You then need to see your supervisor regularly to check out how you are progressing. It is always good to hand in some work for discussion at these meetings. Even if your work is very rough and 'drafty', a supervisor can be so much more help if he or she sees work in progress and what you are and are not managing to do. Then at the end it is good to have some steer on how you are writing up, although in some universities a supervisor may not look at a final draft. One thing that is profoundly unhelpful is to avoid your supervisor right through the process, wait until the last minute and then send him or her a draft of a whole thesis. You get no real help from your supervisor this way – it is far too late to do anything for you. Far better to plan regular meetings right through the process, even if these are by phone or Skype or even email, if you live at a distance.

## Good luck and enjoy!

Writing a dissertation is hard work but it can also be extremely rewarding. You develop new skills, have a great sense of achievement and even become an expert in your own topic. Good luck, and enjoy it.

# References and
# Further Resources

Astley, J. and Francis, L. J. (eds), 2013, *Exploring Ordinary Theology: Everyday Christian Believing and the Church*, Aldershot: Ashgate.

Ballard, P. and Pritchard J., 2006, *Practical Theology in Action,* 2nd edn, London: SPCK.

Barth, K., 1928, *The Word of God and the Word of Man*, trans. Douglas Horton, Boston, Chicago: Pilgrim Press.

Barth, K., 1963, *Evangelical Theology: An Introduction*, trans. Grover Foley, London: Weidenfeld & Nicolson.

Bennett, Z., 2004, *Incorrigible Plurality: Teaching Pastoral Theology in an Ecumenical Context*, Contact Pastoral Monograph No. 14, Edinburgh: Contact Pastoral Trust.

Bennett, Z., 2007, '"Action is the life of all": the praxis-based epistemology of liberation theology', in Rowland, C. (ed.), *Cambridge Companion to Liberation Theology*, 2nd edn, Cambridge: Cambridge University Press, pp. 39–54.

Bennett, Z., '"To see fearlessly, pitifully": what does John Ruskin have to offer to practical theology?', *International Journal of Practical Theology* 14.2 (2011), pp. 189–203.

Bennett, Z., 2013, *Using the Bible in Practical Theology: Historical and Contemporary Perspectives*, Aldershot: Ashgate.

Bennett, Z. and Porumb, R., 'Studying Pastoral Theology in an ecumenical context', *Journal of Adult Theological Education* 8.1 (2011), pp. 38–52.

Bennett Moore, Z., Faltin, L. and Wright, M., 'Critical thinking and international postgraduate students', *Discourse* 3.1 (2003), pp. 63–94.

Bevans, S., 2002, *Models of Contextual Theology*, Maryknoll, NY: Orbis Books.

Boff, C., 1987, *Theology and Praxis: Epistemological Foundations*, Maryknoll, NY: Orbis Books.

Bolton, G., 2010, *Reflective Practice: Writing and Professional Development*, 3rd edn, London: Sage.

Cambridge Theological Federation, *Narrative and Identity*, available at www.theofed.cam.ac.uk/ma_modules/MOD003419.html.

Cameron, H., Bhatti, D., Duce, C. and Sweeney, J., 2010, *Talking about God in Practice: Theological Action Research and Practical Theology*, London: SCM Press.

Cargas, S., Hartley, H., Rowland, C., Sabri, D., Stavrakopulou, F. and Wyatt, J., '"Like a good brisk walk": the relationship between faith stance and academic study in the experience of first year theology students at the University of Oxford', *Discourse* 4.2 (2005), pp. 43–82.

Farley, E., 2000, 'Interpreting situations: an inquiry into the nature of Practical Theology', in Woodward, J. and Pattison, S. (eds), *The Blackwell Reader in Pastoral and Practical Theology*, Oxford: Blackwell, pp. 135–45.

Freire, P., 1972, *Pedagogy of the Oppressed*, tran. Myra Bergman Ramos, Harmondsworth: Penguin.

Gorringe, T. J., 2004, *Furthering Humanity: A Theology of Culture*, Aldershot: Ashgate.

Graham, E. L., 1996, *Transforming Practice: Pastoral Theology in an Age of Uncertainty*, London: Mowbray.

Graham, E., Walton, H. and Ward, F., 2005, *Theological Reflection: Methods*, London: SCM Press.

Green L., 2009, *Let's Do Theology: Resources for Contextual Theology*, 2nd edn, London; New York: Mowbray.

Harrison, B. W., 1990, 'The power of anger in the work of love', in Loades, A. (ed.), *Feminist Theology: A Reader*, London: SPCK, pp. 194–214.

Honey, P. and Mumford, A., 1992, *The Manual of Learning Styles*, 3rd edn, Maidenhead: Peter Honey.

Jillions, J., 'Pastoral theology: reflections from an Orthodox perspective', *British Journal of Theological Education* 13.2 (2003), pp. 161–74.

Kara, H., 2012, *Research and Evaluation for Busy Practitioners: A Time Saving Guide*, Chicago, IL: Policy Press.

Kolb, D., 1984, *Experiential Learning: Experience as the Source of Learning and Development*, Englewood Cliffs: Prentice Hall.

Lash, N., 1988, *Easter in Ordinary: Reflections on Human Experience and the Knowledge of God*, London: SCM Press.

Lartey, E. Y., 2000, 'Practical Theology as a theological form', in Willows, D. and Swinton, J. (eds), *Spiritual Dimensions of Pastoral Care: Practical Theology in a Multidisciplinary Context*, London: Jessica Kingsley, pp. 72–80.

Leach, J., 'Pastoral Theology as Attention', *Contact: Practical Theology and Pastoral Care* 153 (2007), pp. 19–32.

Londonmet, available at http://learning.londonmet.ac.uk/TLTC/learnhigher/Resources/resources/Presentations/Giving%20a%20Presentation.pdf.

Lyall, D., 2000, 'Pastoral action and theological reflection', in Willows, D. and Swinton, J. (eds), *Spiritual Dimensions of Pastoral Care: Practical Theology in a Multidisciplinary Context*, London: Jessica Kingsley, pp. 53–65.

Magister, S., 2008, *Clodovis and Leonardo Boff, Separated Brethren*, available at http://chiesa.espresso.repubblica.it/articolo/205773?eng=y.

Miller-McLemore, B. J., 1999, 'Feminist theory in pastoral theology', in Miller-McLemore, B. J. and Gill-Austern, B. (eds), *Feminist and Womanist Pastoral Theology*, Nashville, TN: Abingdon Press, pp. 77–94.

Moon, J, 2006, *Learning Journals: A Handbook for Reflective Practice and Professional Development*, 2nd edn, Oxford: Routledge.

Moore, P., 'Pastoral theology and spirituality in the pre-Reformation Church', *British Journal of Theological Education* 13.2 (2003), pp. 153–60.

Northcott. M., 2000, 'The case study method in practical theology', in Willows, D. and Swinton, J. (eds), *Spiritual Dimensions of Pastoral Care: Practical Theology in a Multidisciplinary Context*, London: Jessica Kingsley, pp. 59–65.

Orsi, R. A., 2005, *Between Heaven and Earth: The Religious Worlds People Make and the Scholars Who Study Them*, Princeton: Princeton University Press.

Pattison, S., 2000, 'Some straw for the bricks: a basic introduction to theological reflection', in Woodward, J. and Pattison, S. (eds), *The Blackwell Reader in Pastoral and Practical Theology*, Oxford: Blackwell, pp. 136–44.

QAA, 2007, *Theology and Religious Studies*, available at www.qaa.ac.uk/ Publications/InformationAndGuidance/Documents/Theology.pdf.

QAA, 2010, *Master's Degree Characteristics*, The Quality Assurance Agency for Higher Education, available at www.qaa.ac.uk/Publications/InformationAndGuidance/Documents/MastersDegreeCharacteristics.pdf.

Rengert, H., 2013, 'Flourishing freely: investigating senior women church leaders' pastoral sustenance and the implications', MA Dissertation, Anglia Ruskin University.

Ruskin, J., quotations from Ruskin's published works are taken from the Library Edition: Cook, E. T. and Wedderburn, A. (eds), *The Works of John Ruskin*, 39 vols, London: George Allen, 1903–12, referred to as *Works*, volume and page number.

Schön, D., 2003, *The Reflective Practitioner: How Professionals Think in Action*, Aldershot: Ashgate (originally published London: Maurice Temple Smith, 1983).

Siepman, J., 1997, notes to CD Sviatoslav Richter *In Memoriam Legendary Recordings* 1959–65.

Shipani, D., 2011, 'Case Study Method', in Miller-McLemore, B. J. (ed.), *The Wiley-Blackwell Companion to Practical Theology*, Oxford: Wiley-Blackwell.

Soskice, J. M., 1993, 'The truth looks different from here or on seeking the unity of truth from a diversity of perspectives', in Regan, H. and Torrance, A. (eds.), *Christ and Context: The Confrontation between Gospel and Culture*, Edinburgh: T & T Clark, pp. 43–59.

Soskice, J. M., 2007, 'Love and Attention', in Soskice, J. M., *The Kindness of God*, Oxford: Oxford University Press, pp. 7–34.

Soueif, A., 1992, *In the Eye of the Sun*, London: Bloomsbury.

Stott, R., Snaith, A. and Rylance, R. (eds), 2000, *Making your Case: A Practical Guide to Essay Writing*, New York: Longman.

Studyportals, available at www.mastersportal.eu/search/?q=ci-30|di-99|lv-master||8d71f169&sort=name,asc&start=70&length=10.

Turner, M. and Rack, J., 2004, *The Study of Dyslexia*, London: Kluwer Academic/Plenum Publishers.

Vassiliadis, P., no date, *Ecumenical Theological Education: The Task of Orthodox Theology*, available at www.academia.edu/2011820/Ecumenical_Theological_Education._The_Task_of_Orthodox_Theology.

Walton, R., 'Using the Bible and Christian tradition in theological reflection', *British Journal of Theological Education* 13.3 (2003), pp. 133–51.

Willows, D. and Swinton, J. (eds), 2000, *Spiritual Dimensions of Pastoral Care: Practical Theology in a Multidisciplinary Context*, London: Jessica Kingsley.

Woodward, J. and Pattison, S. (eds), 2000, *The Blackwell Reader in Pastoral and Practical Theology*, Oxford: Blackwell Publishers.

Zinsser, W., 2006, *On Writing Well*, 7th edn, New York: Collins.

# Further resources – not already indicated on reference list

## General

Badley, G., 2009, *Write a Lot Better*, Anglia Ruskin University. Part One available at: web.anglia.ac.uk/anet/rdcs/research/info/Write%20a%20 lot%20better%20-%201.pdf. Part Two at web.anglia.ac.uk/anet/rdcs/ research/info/Write%20a%20lot%20better%20-%202.pdf.

The Speak-Write Series of Longman's Study Guides, including:

Stott, R., Young, T. and Bryan, C. (eds), 2001, *Speaking your Mind: Oral Presentation and Seminar Skills*, New York: Longman.

Your own university website.

Other universities, for example two good ones for master's students are:

- www.see.leeds.ac.uk/stepup/skillsarea1.html.
- www.reading.ac.uk/internal/studyadvice/postgraduates/sta-masters studying.aspx.

www.learnhigher.ac.uk/.

www2.open.ac.uk/students/skillsforstudy/postgraduate-study-skills. php.

Royal Literary Fund website: www.rlf.org.uk/index.cfm.

## Distance Learning

Becker, L., 2004, *How to Manage your Distance and Open Learning Course*, Palgrave Study Skills, Basingstoke: Palgrave Macmillan.

Dawson C., 2006, *The Mature Student's Study Guide: Essential Skills for Those Returning to Education or Distance Learning*, 2nd edn, Oxford: How To Books.

## Specific learning difficulties

### Information about specific learning difficulties

Attention Deficit Disorder: The National Attention Deficit Disorder Information and Support Service: www.addiss.co.uk.

Dyslexia Action: http://dyslexiaaction.org.uk/services-and-support.

Dyspraxia Foundation: www.dyspraxiafoundation.org.uk/.

### Disabled Students Allowance

Disabled Students Allowance (England): www.gov.uk/disabled-students-allowances-dsas/overview.

Student Awards Agency for Scotland: www.saas.gov.uk/forms_and_guides/dsa.htm.

### SuperReading

SuperReading: www.superreading.com/.

### Support for students

Association of Dyslexia Specialists in Higher Education: http://adshe.org.uk/.

DnA (Diversity and Ability): www.dnamatters.co.uk/index.html.

## Use of the Bible in theology

Ford, D. and Stanton, G. (eds), 2003, *Reading Texts, Seeking Wisdom: Scripture and Theology*, Grand Rapids, MI: Eerdmans.

Riches, J., 2000, *The Bible: A Very Short Introduction*, Oxford: Oxford University Press.


## For international students

Davies, M., 2011, *Study Skills for International Postgraduates*, Palgrave Study Skills, Basingstoke: Palgrave Macmillan.


## Research methods

Bell, J., 2010, *Doing Your Research Project*, 5th edn, Maidenhead: Open University Press.

Robson, C., 2011, *Real World Research*, 3rd edn, Chichester: Wiley.

Swinton, J. and Mowat, H., 2006, *Practical Theology and Qualitative Research*, London: SCM Press.

Wisker, G., 2001, *The Post-graduate Research Handbook*, Palgrave Study Skills, Basingstoke, Palgrave Macmillan.

# Index